Crisis and Catharsis:
The Power
of the Apocalypse

Crisis and Catharsis: The Power of the Apocalypse

Adela Yarbro Collins

The Westminster Press
Philadelphia

First edition

Published by The Westminster Press®
Philadelphia, Pennsylvania

PRINTED IN THE UNITED STATES OF AMERICA

9 8 7 6 5 4 3 2 1

Library of Congress Cataloging in Publication Data

Collins, Adela Yarbro.
    Crisis and catharsis.

    Includes bibliographical references and index.
    1. Bible. N.T. Revelation—Criticism, interpretation,
etc. I. Title.
BS2825.2.C583   1984   228'.06   83-26084
ISBN 0-664-24521-8 (pbk.)

For
Jesse, Sean, and Aidan

Contents

Acknowledgments

The ideas presented in this book have developed over a period of time and in dialogue with many colleagues. The process began with an invitation from Professor Lars Hartman, on behalf of the organizing committee, to make a presentation on the function of apocalyptic literature at an International Colloquium on Apocalypticism sponsored by the Faculty of Theology at the University of Uppsala in August 1979. Portions of my presentation, which has been published in *Apocalypticism in the Mediterranean World and the Near East,* ed. by David Hellholm (1983), are incorporated here with the permission of J. C. B. Mohr (Paul Siebeck), Tübingen.

My work was given considerable impetus by the opportunity to give the William C. Winslow Lectures at Seabury-Western Theological Seminary in October 1981. I thank my colleagues at Seabury, as well as those at their neighbor seminary, Garrett-Evangelical Theological Seminary, for their support and constructive criticism on that occasion.

Material from my essay "Revelation 18: Taunt-Song or Dirge?" published by J. Duculot, Gembloux, and by Leuven University Press, Louvain, in *L'Apocalypse johannique et l'apocalyptique dans le Nouveau Testament* (Bibliotheca Ephemeridum Theologicarum Lovaniensium, 53), ed. by Jan Lambrecht (1980), pp. 185–204, has been used with permission. The essay was contributed to the Colloquium Biblicum Lovaniense XXX, 1979. Portions of my essay "Myth and History in the Book of Revelation: The Problem of Its Date," published by Eisenbrauns in *Traditions in Transformation: Turning Points in Biblical Faith* (essays presented to Frank M. Cross, Jr.), ed. by Baruch Halpern and Jon D. Levenson (1981), have been used with permission.

I wish to express my gratitude to McCormick Theological Seminary for study leaves in 1979 and 1982, during which I worked on this project, and for the Seminary's help in producing the manuscript. Special thanks go to Doran Hill and Elizabeth Watson for typing the manuscript.

Abbreviations

AB	Anchor Bible
ANRW	H. Temporini and W. Haase (eds.), *Aufstieg und Niedergang der römischen Welt*
BR	*Biblical Research*
CAH	*Cambridge Ancient History*
CBQ	*Catholic Biblical Quarterly*
HTR	*Harvard Theological Review*
ICC	International Critical Commentary
IDB	G. A. Buttrick (ed.), *Interpreter's Dictionary of the Bible*
IDBSup	Supplementary volume to *IDB*
JBL	*Journal of Biblical Literature*
LCL	Loeb Classical Library
LSJ	Liddell-Scott-Jones, *Greek-English Lexicon*
NTS	*New Testament Studies*
OCD	*Oxford Classical Dictionary,* 1949
PW	Pauly-Wissowa, *Real-Encyclopädie der classischen Altertumswissenschaft*
RSR	*Recherches de science religieuse*
TLZ	*Theologische Literaturzeitung*
TU	Texte und Untersuchungen
ZNW	*Zeitschrift für die neutestamentliche Wissenschaft*

Introduction

The book of Revelation usually awakens either passionate commitment or puzzlement. Traditional evangelicals or fundamentalists are passionately committed to a particular way of reading the work. They disagree among themselves on the details, but share a basic approach. The assumption is that the book of Revelation, supplemented by a few other portions of the Bible, contains a systematic doctrine of the last things. This doctrine is rational in the sense that there are no awkward gaps or contradictions. The picture of the future is clear. Revelation, they assume, refers to objective, actually existing heavenly beings and places and to events that will occur on the historical plane. Most strikingly, they believe that biblical prophecy refers not to the time of the biblical writers themselves, but to the twentieth century.

Millions of evangelicals believe that Jesus will return before the end of this century to establish his thousand-year reign on earth. A book proclaiming this message, Hal Lindsey's *The Late Great Planet Earth,* sold more copies in the 1970s than any other work of nonfiction, making him perhaps the best-selling author of the decade. The puzzle of 666 (Rev. 13:18) continues to fascinate and to inspire ingenious solutions. Sometimes this mysterious number is interpreted as a reference to a personal Antichrist or False Messiah. Mussolini, Hitler, Henry Kissinger, and Anwar Sadat have been so identified in this century. At other times the number is taken as a real numerical code that is being subtly pushed on the people of the world to prepare them for the appearance of the Antichrist. In a kind of eschatological panic, it has been claimed that products from the Republic of China, the United States, and other countries have been marked with 666 as their product code.[1] It is also supposed to be a common prefix in computer programs of large department stores and international institutions.

Eschatological excitement and a certain fearfulness is thus aroused in relation to computerization, identification numbers of all sorts, and even cable television. In expectation of a speedy end, some evangelical Protestants and charismatic Catholics have moved to rural areas, sometimes founding new communities, to await the return of Christ. Others have suffered financial embarrassment because they took out loans that they never expected to have to repay.

This approach to Revelation has ancient roots. It is in fact the oldest-known interpretation, which was widespread in both the Eastern and Western regions of the church in the second and third centuries. The Montanists provide a vivid example. They began a prophetic renewal, involving direct, new inspiration of individuals by the Holy Spirit. The movement began in Phrygia, just east of the seven cities of the Apocalypse. One of the leaders announced the revelation that the heavenly Jerusalem would descend near the village of Pepuza, in their own region. The current version of this approach is a modern revival with roots in nineteenth-century England.

Some hold the conservative evangelical position because it is the tradition in which they grew up. Others adopt it because it provides a symbolic universe within which they can live and because it meets certain felt or unconscious needs. A great many Americans are left completely cold by the traditional evangelical approach, however, because it flies in the face of their assumptions about the nature of the Bible and reality. Some of these nonevangelicals have been introduced to the historical-critical approach in Christian education in the mainline churches or in religious studies courses in colleges or universities.

The historical-critical approach to the Bible blossomed in the nineteenth century, under the influence of the modern science of historiography. The focus was on the author of a particular text, the intended readers, and the historical situation in which they lived, which shaped the text and was addressed by it. Revelation came to be seen, not as a prophecy of the modern reader's future, but as a response to Roman persecution of Christians near the end of the first century. Obviously, such an approach created some distance between the modern readers and the text. Some saw this distance as a good thing because, from the point of view of a historically sensitive person, it reflected the real state of affairs. Many in the nineteenth century and up to the present day have found this approach to be a breath of fresh air in an ecclesiastical context stifled by rigid dogmatism. Some critics of the method have been dismayed at the gap it often creates between believer and text, between their two worlds. It has seemed that the greater the historical knowledge and imagination employed in studying a text, the harder it is to relate the text to the world of the believing interpreter and to the church. Much of the reason for this result is that the historical-critical approach is more interested in origins than in the history of the effects of a text; more concerned with differences between the text's world and the interpreter's world than with similarities.

The historical-critical method has not always been a purely negative approach, however. Some practitioners of the method and many (such as theologians and preachers) who make use of its results have been able effectively to build bridges from the historical situation of the text to the interpreter's situation. This bridging activity has usually involved finding analogies. While it is recognized that each historical situation is, strictly speaking, unique, there are similarities between past and present because of recurrent human experiences, like birth and death, love and hatred, and the desire for immortality. The exploitative use of power by some against others is another common human experience, one that finds powerful expression in the book of Revelation and which has moved many to apply it to their own situations.

The historical-critical approach has lost influence in the last two decades, not so much because of its negative function as because of the growing perception that it is too limited a tool in the search for the meaning of a text. The great fascination with historical consciousness and historical relativity is waning for some because it is so much taken for granted. Newer, and in some cases more radically critical, theories now seem to have greater explanatory power.

Some interpreters seek not so much to explain as to understand. Many of these have learned from aesthetic literary critics and adapted some of their methods for biblical study. Recent research on the parables of Jesus as metaphorical narrative is an example of this process. This approach is often able to make a text accessible and meaningful to the modern reader, but it loses credibility when the historical context is not taken seriously.

Biblical critics have learned a great deal from literary critics, philosophers, and others on the subjects of symbol and myth. Bridge-building from this perspective can be difficult. For many of the laity, these are inferior categories. People are apt to say "only a symbol" and to equate myth with falsehood. In part this attitude is due to the continuing tendency in popular American culture to place a high value on fact, the visible world, and logical or empirical proof. Perhaps on a deeper level it is due to the reluctance of the average person to admit that his or her life is founded on something less absolute than bedrock.

If people are courageous enough, analogies can easily be found between traditional symbols and myths and elements that have a similar role to play in modern life. Although a modern person may have different opinions from an ancient or traditional person about what is real, there are still certain ideas or theories that serve most moderns as a point of orientation for experiences and life. For some it may be an idea or theory that had its origin in empirical science, but which has come to have a comprehensive and deep function for which it was not necessarily intended, and which in any case goes beyond the limited purposes of empirical science. Scientific theories that have become myths for many individuals are the theory of evolution and Freudian psychoanalytic theory. Such theories are like myths when they provide people with a symbolic universe in which they find meaning and personal significance.

Others take their symbolic bearings from literature, perhaps from the great tragedies of the Greeks and Shakespeare. Some, perhaps quite unconsciously, order their lives, or indeed escape from their lives, in terms of heroes, heroines, and mythic patterns of popular American literature, films, and television. People who are sensitive to the provisional and partial character of scientific theories or who are self-conscious about their own reliance on myth are more able to take myth and symbol seriously as categories for interpreting the Bible.

Certain interpreters of the Bible have turned to newer and less established social sciences than history—namely, sociology, psychology, and anthropology—for promising approaches in the quest for the meaning of texts. Some of these approaches are more radical than the original form of the historical-critical method. One reason for their radical character is that some generative insights underlying them came from thinkers who saw religion either as a limited phase in human history or an outright weakness to be eliminated, thinkers like Feuerbach, Marx, Nietzsche, and Freud. These men proposed theories that explained the origin and function of religious symbols that bypassed the conscious intention and self-understanding of the author of a text or the typical believer. Their interpretations go "behind" or "beneath" conscious attitudes to what are considered to be deeper realities. Feuerbach argued that humanity had projected its best qualities outward in conceiving the idea of God, qualities that had to be reclaimed; theology must become anthropology. Marx claimed that religion was an ideology that legitimated unequal distribution of wealth. Nietzsche interpreted religious language as an instrument in the struggle for survival and power. Freud argued that religion was an illusion, in the sense that it was the expression of wishes, wishes rooted in human instincts and the experiences of early childhood. Nietzsche recommended that the reader of texts cultivate the "art of mistrust" as a means of uncovering the "false consciousness" by which all human beings deceive themselves about their true motives.

Another factor that makes socioscientifically based interpretations of religion seem radical is their affinity with relativism. The critical study of history showed how different one epoch is from another and how the ideas and decisions of persons are limited by their historical circumstances. The so-called historicists, for example, Wilhelm Dilthey, argued that all human thought is historically relative; that is, it is virtually determined by its historical situation. Some interpreters of religion from a socioscientific perspective, for example, recent theorists of the "sociology of knowledge," have accepted the historicist thesis of relativism. The result has been that the question of the ultimate validity or truth of religious behavior, claims, and texts is set aside. Religious symbols are treated as human constructions and are studied in relation to their sociohistorical situation or "social location."[2] A text like the book of Revelation would be studied by seeking to discover how it emerged in the interaction between objective and subjective social reality and how it then influenced both of those dimensions. Such a theoretical framework has an affinity with the philosophical position that all theories are human constructions that are at best partial truths. Reality in itself is unknowable.

Approaches to religion that are socioscientific in a thoroughgoing way have been criticized as reductionist; that is, as reducing one form of knowledge (theology) to another (economics, sociology, psychology, or anthropology). On a more sophisticated level, Paul Ricoeur has argued that the "distinctive uses of language [such] as science, poetry, ordinary discourse, psychoanalytic discourse, religous discourse, etc." are fundamentally and qualitatively different from one another and thus may not be combined in a single interpretative system. Because of this conviction he regards the interpretations of religion by Marx, Nietzsche, and Freud as "reductive endeavors" when they attempt to "reduce religous language to ideology, to resentment, or to obsessive neurosis," respectively.[3] Ricoeur has described Freudian psychoanalysis as a "hermeneutic of suspicion." He would presumably extend the term to include the approach of interpreters of religion who practice Nietzsche's "art of mistrust." Ricoeur has called instead for a "hermeneutic of belief."[4] Recognizing that a theory like psychoanalysis can expose the illusions of consciousness, he nevertheless rejects the naturalism of Freud and concludes that certain symbols and myths can, if properly interpreted, lead humanity on to its limits. Belief is listening to the call, hearing the kerygma addressed to the one who has discovered how certain myths speak to the broken human condition.

But in what theoretical framework or against what background ought the symbols and myths in biblical texts to be interpreted? The classic historical-critical approach interpreted a text by trying to reconstruct the intention of the author in writing it. This historiographical ideal influenced literary critics as well as biblical scholars, with the result that the details of Shakespeare's life were seen for a time as crucial in understanding his plays. That approach lost influence because of the argument made in the "new criticism" that the author's intention does not exhaust the meaning of a text. Similar criticisms have been made in biblical studies of the tendency to give full explanatory power to the author's intention.

A rather extreme form of that criticism was made by Ricoeur in his book *Interpretation Theory: Discourse and the Surplus of Meaning:*

> Not the intention of the author, which is supposed to be hidden behind the text; not the historical situation common to the author and his original readers; not the expectations or feelings of these original readers; not even their understanding of themselves as historical and cultural phenomena. What has to be appropriated is the meaning of the text itself, conceived in a dynamic way as the direction of thought opened up by the text. In other words, what has to be appropriated is nothing other than the power of disclosing a world that constitutes the reference of the text. In this way we are as far as possible from the Romanticist ideal of coinciding with a foreign psyche. If we may be said to coincide with anything, it is not the inner life of another ego, but the disclosure of a possible way of looking at things, which is the genuine referential power of the text.[5]

Ricoeur concludes that the effort to get behind the text to what the author intended to say is misdirected. This conclusion is based on the argument that when speech becomes text, the text is cut loose from its original situation. By using the medium of writing rather than oral speech, the author sets up a barrier to the readers' knowledge of the original act of discourse. This barrier does not permit the interpreter to rush to the question of the text's contemporary relevance. The horizon of the text should not be confined to the interpreter's own horizon. The interpreter must allow the world of the text to be strange and must keep in mind that true understanding is understanding at a distance. The two pitfalls of Romanticist hermeneutics and hasty application can be avoided, according to Ricoeur, by directing attention to the "world" that is "before" or "in front of" the text. This is the "world" or "way of looking at things" disclosed by the text. It is this world which is the intermediate link between the past of the author and the present of the interpreter. The text presents or proposes a world of its own, which has its own structure, its own symbolic coherence, and a capacity to generate audiences of its own.[6]

I would agree that full explanatory power should not be given to the author's intention. What the writer *intended to say* and what he or she actually *said* may not always fully coincide. I would also agree that a text has its own symbolic coherence, that it proposes a way of looking at things. By being committed to writing and being preserved and circulated beyond its original situation, a text is, in a sense, cut loose from the existential, historical situation in which it emerged. When we read Paul's first letter to the Corinthians, we do not know what he had said to them orally on visits that predated the letter, and we do not have immediate access to their shared assumptions. But we can attempt to reconstruct these things as historians. We cannot have certainty about them, but we can generate hypotheses and judge which are more and which are less likely. If we do not engage in such historical reconstruction, we may fail to understand or may misunderstand the text.

When a text is regarded as absolutely cut off from its original situation, the "world of the text" becomes, if it was not so already, multivalent. That is, the text does not propose a single, straightforward way of looking at things, or even a single direction of thought. Rather, it is open to a probably infinite range of possible interpretations. Some theorists of interpretation, like Hans-Georg Gadamer, would say that most if not all of these interpretations have their own validity.[7] Others, like E. D. Hirsch, would argue that the meaning of a text must be linked to the situation in which it emerged. Interpretations that do not take the original historical context seriously express the *significance* of the text to various readers, but cannot claim to express its normative *meaning* or range of meanings.[8]

I side with Hirsch on this issue. The symbolic universe of every text is shaped by its historical context and cultural milieu. Bruno Bettelheim has argued persuasively that fairy tales have a psychological function; that is, they help children—and sometimes adolescents and adults—sort out and come to terms with deep fears and anxieties.[9] Even if he is right about their function, the modern reader cannot fail to notice that fairy tales bear the marks of their cultural origin. To take a simple example, American children of the 1980s need an explanation of spinning and spinning wheels. The tales also reflect the cultural phenomena of monarchy and patriarchy. To ignore these factors is to limit understanding and perhaps to allow oneself uncritically to be shaped by a text.

Further, there ought to be a normative range of meanings in order to distinguish more- and less-adequate interpretations. Even if every interpretation is determined by its historical setting or social location, there is still the possibility of judging one interpretation superior to another from the same cultural context. There is also an ethical consideration. If one interpretation is as valid as another, responsible people have fewer resources for exposing vicious propaganda. If there are no limits on the possible interpretations of the beast in Revelation, a human group, such as the Jews, can be victimized more easily and with apparent biblical sanction.

It makes some sense to speak of a text as an intermediate link between the past of the author and the present of the interpreter, because the text has a certain objective character. One cannot say with any credibility, for example, that the supreme value expressed in Revelation is the survival of physical life. There are certain things a text cannot be made to say. But that objective quality is limited. The connotations of words and the evocative power of symbols and myths cannot be determined by reading an isolated text in a vacuum. The logic, the sense of a text, is discovered only when it is read in terms of a specific culture, specific historical circumstances, a particular point of view. If this point of view is not a reconstruction of the original context of the text, it will inevitably be the cultural perspective of the interpreter, perhaps as shaped by some powerful interpretation between the author's and the interpreter's time.

It must be clear by now that I regard careful attention to the original historical context as the essential foundation of the interpretation of any text. Such attention is especially important for the book of Revelation, since it alludes, though at times in a veiled way, to historical, political, economic, and social conditions of its time. Further, the underlying questions of the book and its very message are deeply political. Without a precise knowledge of the book's setting, the interpreter is in danger of serious misunderstanding. Therefore, I am forced to disagree with Ricoeur's judgment that the author's intention and the historical situation common to the author and his original readers are not essential elements in the interpretation of a text. Historical-critical method and the historian's perspective thus underlie and permeate the present volume. They are dominant especially in Chapter 1, "Who Wrote the Book of Revelation?" and in

Chapter 2, "When Was Revelation Written?" which establish the framework for the other interpretative approaches taken in other chapters.

Although I believe that historical methods are essential, I do not think that they are fully adequate to the task of exploring the mystery of the meaning of a text. Classic historiographical methods have focused on the conscious intentions and attitudes of authors and original readers. Certain great thinkers of the recent past, especially Marx, Nietzsche, and Freud, have shown us that much of what we do and say has functions of which we are unconscious, and that we are easily able to deceive ourselves about reality. Sociology and anthropology focus on the unconscious functions of human behavior and language. If we are to be responsible interpreters, we must take these newer insights into account and ask what light sociological and anthropological theories are able to cast on sociohistorical data. This task is taken up in Chapter 3, "The Social Situation—Perceived Crisis," and Chapter 4, "Social Radicalism in the Apocalypse." In these chapters certain cross-cultural theories about the origins and causes of "crisis cults" or apocalyptic movements are tested in the light of the social setting and function of the book of Revelation. The major examples of such theories are those which argue for social crisis as the cause of apocalyptic movements, and those which see in such movements an attempt to compensate for a lack of wealth, status, or power.

The book of Revelation is not only an artifact from a specific place and time, a historical document; it is also a literary creation, a work of great artistic beauty and power. As aesthetic literary critics and philosophers have reminded us so often, a great work of literary art has a dynamic union of form and content. The content or message is best grasped in and through the form. Thus the historical approach must be complemented also by literary sensitivity and by aesthetic literary-critical methods. In the first part of Chapter 5, "The Power of Apocalyptic Rhetoric—Catharsis," a study of the artful use of myth and symbol is offered to show how Revelation achieved its effect on the original readers. The literary effect of Revelation can best be seen with its historical setting in mind.

The third of the newer social sciences, psychology, has awakened widespread enthusiasm and fascination in our century, and is increasingly doing so among interpreters of the Bible. Psychological theories have such an appeal in part because they explain behavior that is puzzling. The book of Revelation has often been interpreted psychologically and usually seen as pathological in some way. It is my contention that certain psychological theories, such as Freudian reflections on aggression, Rollo May's theories about power, and Ernest Becker's theories about the denial of death, are strikingly illuminating for Revelation. Building on the previous historical, sociological, and literary studies, the second part of Chapter 5 examines Revelation from a psychological point of view. I do not attempt to psychoanalyze the author; there are insufficient data to do so, even if it were desirable and I were capable. The approach is rather to indicate the probable sociopsychological origins and functions that the text had.

It is evident that I am practicing Nietzsche's art of mistrust. It is not because I believe that the author of Revelation was intentionally deceptive or that he was a psychopathic personality. It is rather because he was human like the rest of us. Every text can be read in three different ways: precritically, critically, and postcritically. A precritical reading is naive, spontaneous, not reflected upon. The precritical reader is personally involved in a text in a way based on unconscious preferences, motives, and processes of socialization. The precritical reader is usually a gullible reader, one who accepts and believes the text at face value and applies it directly and simply to himself or herself. The critical reader is detached, self-conscious, reflective, and analytical. Such a reader seeks reasons, explanations, and evidence. An attempt is made to examine both the self and the text with objectivity, from a distance. The fundamentalist reading of Revelation is a precritical reading. What this book attempts to do is provide the occasion for a critical reading of the text of Revelation. Getting "behind" the text, with the help of history, sociology, anthropology, and especially psychology, is a crucial element in a critical reading. I do not do this in the arrogant illusion of having fewer illusions than the author of Revelation. I do it because I recognize in the text human impulses I feel in myself and see in my neighbors; because being critical of the writer of Revelation helps me be more critical of myself. I hope that the reader of this book will also reap the benefit of greater self-awareness.

A postcritical reading of a text is one based on a lived, experienced knowledge of the text as a product of another time and place and as a flawed human product. At the same time there is openness to a personal reinvolvement on a new level. There is recognition that a flawed, broken myth can still speak to our broken human condition. In the conclusion I will explore the possibilities for a postcritical reading of Revelation in the twentieth century.

NOTES

1. Mary Stewart Relfe, *The New Money System "666"* (Montgomery, Ala.: Ministries, Inc., 1982).

2. Peter L. Berger and Thomas Luckmann, *The Social Construction of Reality* (Doubleday & Co., 1966), especially the Introduction and Conclusion.

3. Paul Ricoeur, *Essays on Biblical Interpretation,* ed. by Lewis S. Mudge (Fortress Press, 1980), pp. 42–43.

4. Ibid., pp. 14–15.

5. Paul Ricoeur, *Interpretation Theory: Discourse and the Surplus of Meaning* (Texas Christian University Press, 1976), p. 92.

6. Paul Ricoeur, *Philosophical Hermeneutics and Theological Hermeneutics: Ideology, Utopia and Faith* (Berkeley: Center for Hermeneutical Studies in Hellenistic and Modern Culture, 1976).

7. Hans-Georg Gadamer, *Truth and Method* (Seabury Press, 1975).

8. E. D. Hirsch, *Validity in Interpretation* (Yale University Press, 1967).

9. Bruno Bettelheim, *The Uses of Enchantment* (Random House, 1975).

1
Who Wrote the Book of Revelation?

As suggested in the Introduction, knowledge of the historical setting of the book of Revelation is crucial in any attempt to understand or interpret it responsibly. Although reconstructing the author's intention is not a complete explanation of a literary work, it is nevertheless an essential feature that helps distinguish merely possible meanings from probable meanings of the text. This chapter lays a foundation for the task of determining the author's intention and for other related facets of Revelation's historical situation by seeking to answer the question, Who wrote the book of Revelation?

THE HISTORICAL QUEST

The earliest writer to be familiar with the book of Revelation, as far as we know, was Papias. He was bishop of Hierapolis, a town not far from Laodicea, one of the seven towns to which Revelation was addressed. Papias was active in the early part of the second century. He wrote a work called *Interpretations of Sayings of the Lord,* which has been lost since the ninth century, but which was cited by many ancient writers.[1] According to Andreas of Caesarea, who wrote a commentary on Revelation in the sixth century, Papias knew the book, considered it to be divinely inspired, and commented on at least one passage.[2] Papias, however, apparently made no clear statement about the authorship. Justin Martyr, who resided for a time in Ephesus, another of the seven cities of the Apocalypse, around 135 C.E., says in his *Dialogue with Trypho* that the book of Revelation was written by John, one of the apostles of Christ.

Irenaeus is the earliest known writer to attribute both the book of Revelation and the Gospel of John to John the son of Zebedee.

Irenaeus was a native of Asia Minor who spent his youth in Smyrna, another of the Apocalypse's seven cities. His middle and later life were spent in Lyons, in Gaul (modern France). He also visited Rome. His major work, *Refutation of Gnosis Falsely So Called,* was written in Greek about 180 C.E. It is usually referred to by the Latin title, *Adversus Haereses.* Other major figures in the early church, Hippolytus, Tertullian, and Origen, apparently followed Irenaeus in their judgments on the authorship of the two works. Their testimony shaped the majority opinion until the rise of historical-critical biblical scholarship. A considerable number of more conservative scholars still hold the same opinion today. Apart from the merits of the evidence, there has been a strong desire to affirm the church's tradition —in part, at least, because of the fear that if the tradition is wrong on this point, it may be wrong on other, more central points as well.[3]

It seems at first thought quite reasonable to trust Justin and Irenaeus as reliable authorities. Justin was living in one of the seven cities only about forty years after the traditional date of the composition of Revelation. Irenaeus says that as a child he heard Polycarp talk about his conversations with John and with the others who had seen the Lord. In another place he says that he had traditions from all the presbyters (or elders) who had met in Asia with John, the disciple of the Lord.[4]

But there are a number of good reasons for doubting the accuracy of the opinions of Justin and Irenaeus on the authorship of the book of Revelation. No one reason is compelling as a single argument, but their cumulative weight shifts the balance of probability away from the authorship of John the son of Zebedee. If that John wrote Revelation, he must have done so at a very advanced age (assuming again that the traditional date, given by Irenaeus, is correct; that is, about 95 or 96 C.E.). He would have been at least eighty years old by that time. A number of texts from a wide variety of times and places suggest that John the son of Zebedee was martyred (or died in some other manner) probably before 70 C.E.[5] These texts attest a Christian tradition in conflict with the one first found in full form in Irenaeus. It is of course possible to harmonize the two and to argue that John was martyred at a very advanced age, but such a hypothesis is not very likely.

The author of the book of Revelation does indeed refer to himself as "John," but not in such a way as to point clearly to John the son of Zebedee. The name John (Greek, *Iōannēs;* Hebrew, *Yohanan*) was common among Jews from the exile onward, and among the early Christians.[6] The author of Revelation never refers to himself as an apostle or a disciple of the Lord. In the vision of the new Jerusalem, the twelve names of the twelve apostles of the Lamb are seen inscribed on the twelve foundations of the wall around the city (21:14). The implication is that the church in the author's time prefigures the heavenly Jerusalem or is its earthly counterpart. The saying reflects a situation in which the time of the apostles is past. It is unlikely that a living apostle would speak in such a way. Revelation 21:14 has more in common with the post-Pauline Eph. 2:20 than with Paul's own remarks in 1 Cor. 3:10–15.

Some have argued that the book of Revelation is pseudonymous; that is, that it was written by someone who wanted the readers to think that it was composed by John, the son of Zebedee. The first to take this position were evidently a group in Asia Minor who opposed the Montanist movement in the second century. The Montanists claimed that the promise of the Paraclete in the Gospel of John had been fulfilled in their midst. They spoke oracles of God and the Spirit in the first person and expected the heavenly Jerusalem (Revelation 21) to descend near Pepuza, a village in Phrygia, the home of the movement. Phrygia, as we have said, was a region just east of the seven cities of the Apocalypse. The group that opposed the Montanists was called the Alogi by Epiphanius, and he says that according to them the book of Revelation was written by Cerinthus.[7] According to Eusebius, Cerinthus was a heretic who looked forward to an earthly, sensual kingdom of Christ.[8] Irenaeus says that he was a contemporary of John in Ephesus.[9] Somewhat later, a presbyter in Rome named Gaius, who was a contemporary of the bishop Zephyrinus (202–219), also led a movement against the Montanists. Part of his attack involved the claim that the book of Revelation, which they revered and used, was not an apostolic book but a false writing by Cerinthus.

The hypothesis that the book is pseudonymous is one way of explaining how two books as different as the Apocalypse and the Gospel of John could be attributed to the same author. It is not a very likely hypothesis, however. If the book of Revelation were pseudonymous, the author would probably have taken more care that the readers would make the correct identification. The pastoral epistles, for example, do not simply use the name Paul. They refer also to Paul's preferred self-designation, "an apostle of Christ Jesus" (1 Tim. 1:1; 2 Tim. 1:1; see also Titus 1:1). These pseudonymous letters also contain allusions to events in Paul's life and other personal remarks, for example about Paul's imprisonment (1 Tim. 1:8). The beginning of the pseudonymous Jewish apocalypse of Ezra was perhaps changed by the Christian editor. The new, Christian form of the book begins with Ezra's genealogy (2 Esdr. 1:1–3). The Jewish apocalypse apparently ended with a legend of the reproduction of the books of the law, which allegedly had been destroyed along with the temple, and the production of certain secret books by divine power through Ezra. This legend fits the historical character of the scribe Ezra who expounded and administered the divine law in the early period of the restoration.

There is nothing comparable to these features in the book of Revelation. The author does not refer to himself as apostle or disciple of the Lord. There are no autobiographical or legendary elements to link him to the person of John the son of Zebedee. When he speaks of the twelve apostles of the Lamb (21:14), there is nothing to indicate that he was supposed to be a member of that group. The self-presentation of the author of Revelation is not in the style of a pseudonymous writer.

Irenaeus' opinion that the Gospel and the Apocalypse were written by the same person is untenable. Historical-critical scholarship has marshaled a great deal of evidence against the supposition. Some excellent arguments against common authorship were already put forward by Dionysius, bishop of Alexandria in Egypt in the second half of the third century. He was led to examine the issue because he, as an allegorist in the manner of Origen, who inclined toward spiritual interpretations, was critical of a movement in a neighboring region that involved an earthly messianic reign of a thousand years, characterized, for example, by an abundance of wine. This is the same kind of millenarianism that Cerinthus apparently held. Unlike the Alogi and Gaius, Dionysius did not claim that Revelation was pseudonymous. He claimed that he did not wish to set it aside, since it was so highly esteemed by many in the church. He did, however, raise doubts about its authority. Dionysius assumed that the Gospel was indeed by John the son of Zebedee and argued that both works could not be. Thus, he concluded, Revelation must be by some other man by the name John. In spite of Dionysius' statement that the Apocalypse was by a holy and inspired man, it lost influence in the East. Its sacred status was disputed officially until Athanasius supported its inclusion among the sacred books in 367 C.E.[10]

Dionysius pointed out that the Gospel and epistles attributed to John are anonymous, whereas the author of Revelation names himself. He also noted that the Greek of the Gospel and first epistle is correct and elegant, while that of the Apocalypse is inaccurate and even barbarous.[11] The Renaissance humanist Erasmus revived the arguments against common authorship of the Gospel of John and

Revelation. J. S. Semler, one of the pioneering historical-critical scholars, rejected the tradition that the apostle John wrote the Apocalypse because of its theology and position in the history of religions.[12]

Like Semler, the Tübingen school of New Testament scholarship, led by Ferdinand Christian Baur, which flourished from about 1826 to 1860, focused on matters of content. They argued that the two books could not have been written by the same person because of the radical difference in theological perspective. In particular, they suggested that no one could hold firmly both to the fulfilled hope expressed in the Gospel with its emphasis on present salvation and also to the intense expectation of future salvation in the Apocalypse.[13]

The arguments of Dionysius, Semler, and the Tübingen school, which were expanded and refined by later critics, seriously call Irenaeus' reliability into question on the issue of authorship.[14] A second, more critical look at Irenaeus supports the conclusion that he, and probably Justin as well, was mistaken on this matter. He obviously confused James the apostle with James the brother of the Lord and wrongly claimed that Papias was a disciple of John the apostle. Irenaeus is not alone among writers of the second century in making mistakes about figures of the first century. Polycrates, bishop of Ephesus, in a letter written to the bishop of Rome in about 190 C.E., confused Philip the apostle (Mark 3:18) with Philip the evangelist (that is, the deacon; Acts 6:1–5; 8:4–8, 12–13, 26–40; 21:8). Papias apparently made the same mistake, although he lived in the town where Philip the evangelist eventually died (Hierapolis).[15] Given the fact that certain names (such as John) were very common, the potential for confusion, especially a few generations later, was very great. There was also a tendency to associate revered and widely used books with apostolic authors. The underlying criteria for acceptance were soundness of content and widespread use in the church. If these were present, the assumption was that the authorship must be apostolic. On the other hand, if the content was suspect, apostolic authorship was challenged.[16]

Naturally enough, once doubt is raised about John the son of Zebedee being the author, curiosity is aroused about who the author actually was. If the work is not pseudonymous, the writer must be someone by the name of John, perhaps otherwise known. Dionysius of Alexandria, after excluding John the son of Zebedee from consideration, speculated that the author of Revelation could be John surnamed Mark, who is mentioned in Acts 13:5 as the assistant of Paul and Barnabas. But, as Dionysius noted, John Mark is explicitly said to have traveled with Paul and Barnabas only from Jerusalem to

Antioch and from there to Cyprus. When the company of Paul sailed from the island of Cyprus to the coast of Asia Minor, John Mark returned to Jerusalem (Acts 13:13). According to Papias, John Mark wrote a Gospel (Mark) based upon the apostle Peter's teaching and memories.[17] Clement of Alexandria says that John Mark founded the church in Alexandria.[18] Dionysius rejected his own hypothesis because Acts does not say that John Mark went to Asia. Since there is no reliable tradition linking John Mark to western Asia Minor and no other positive reason for linking him with the Apocalypse, we should certainly follow Dionysius in eliminating him as a likely candidate.

Dionysius concluded that the author must be another John in Asia, perhaps one named after the apostle.[19] In support of this conclusion, he mentioned that there are two monuments (presumably intended to mark tombs) at Ephesus and that both bear the name John. We know these arguments of Dionysius because Eusebius quoted them. In another context, in which Eusebius comments on the work of Papias, he gives his own opinion on the matter. He first quotes Papias as to his sources:

> But if anyone came who had followed the presbyters, I was accustomed to inquire about the sayings of the presbyters, what Andrew or what Peter had said, or Philip or Thomas or Jacob or John or Matthew or any other of the Lord's disciples; and what Aristion and the presbyter John, the disciples of the Lord, say. For I do not regard that which comes from books as so valuable for myself as that which comes from a living and abiding voice.[20]

Eusebius points out that two Johns are named here. He argues that the first group of disciples of the Lord who are mentioned are apostles (Andrew and Peter, Philip through Matthew). The John included in this group, according to Eusebius, is the evangelist. Since the second John is mentioned with Aristion, who was evidently not one of the twelve, and since he is clearly designated as a presbyter (or elder), Eusebius concludes that the second "John" refers not to the apostle, John the son of Zebedee, but to another John. He links Papias' evidence for two Johns in Asia with the statement (probably of Dionysius) that there were two tombs called John's in Ephesus. Eusebius then concludes that if John the son of Zebedee did not see the Revelation, then John the presbyter probably did.

Although this reasoning is hardly cogent, a large number of modern scholars have concluded that John the presbyter was either the actual or the pseudonymous author of Revelation. Many of the trailblazing German scholars of the late nineteenth and early twentieth centuries, such as Johannes Weiss and Wilhelm Bousset, held this view. The English scholar Henry Swete, writing in 1909, could say: "The Apocalypse is now ascribed to the Elder by perhaps a majority of critics."[21] It must, however, be noted that the author of John never presents himself as a presbyter (or elder) or as a disciple of the Lord. He thus does not use in his self-designation the two terms that figure prominently in Papias' remarks. It should also be noted that Papias himself does not say that John the presbyter lived in Ephesus or even in Asia Minor for any length of time. He also, of course, does not claim that this John wrote the Apocalypse. Thus more recent scholarship, represented by W. G. Kümmel, has tended to reject the hypothesis that the author of Revelation was John the presbyter.[22]

In the recent commentary in the Anchor Bible series, J. M. Ford argued that the authority behind the book of Revelation is John the Baptist.[23] She tried to demonstrate that chs. 4–11 reflect the Baptist's messianic expectation quite directly, and that chs. 12–22, although from a somewhat later date, still reflect the expectations of his disciples, who may or may not have become Christians. Only chs. 1–3 and a few verses in ch. 22 are surely Christian in her view; she suggests that these were added by a disciple of John the Baptist, who perhaps had come to know Jesus Christ more accurately, like the followers of John mentioned in Acts 19 or like Apollos, mentioned in Acts 18:24–28.

This theory is not persuasive. It is based on the assumption that Revelation is a compilation of sources. That view was very popular in the last quarter of the nineteenth century. But toward the end of the century, Bousset argued cogently for the essential unity of the book based on its consistency in language and style. Somewhat later R. H. Charles demonstrated this essential unity in great detail. Ford's theory is problematic also because it ignores the Christian character of the book as a whole. One may dispute whether it truly preaches Christ, as Luther did, but it is quite clear that the author considered himself a follower of Christ. Only by arbitrarily eliminating references to the Lamb, its death, and its redeeming blood, or by interpreting them in a strained way, can the Christian character of even chs. 4–11 be denied. Thus any sort of attribution of Revelation to John the Baptist is incompatible with the evidence.

Because of the difficulty in ascribing two books so different in language and theology as the Gospel of John and Revelation to a single writer, various theories have risen about their relationship. In spite of their differences, many scholars have held to the view that they go back to a single author. Some have argued that the differences are simply a matter of literary form. Since one is a Gospel and the other a type of revelatory literature, they naturally have different subject matter, vocabulary, and perspectives. One looks to the past, to the earthly life of Jesus; the other, to the heavenly world and to the future. The argument is not persuasive, however, because the differences are more extensive and deeper than a difference in genre can explain. Different words are used to refer to the same thing; for example, the two books use different words for lamb and for Jerusalem.[24]

Another approach is to interpret the theological and eschatological perspectives of the two works in such a way as to emphasize their similarities and minimize their differences. Such an approach is appropriate for one who as a theologian wishes to construct a Johannine theology or a biblical theology. It is not appropriate for a historian. It overlooks the acute differences in emphasis and thus what is really distinctive and characteristic of each book.

Others have suggested that the two books were written at different times and that their differences are due to the author's changed ideas and attitudes as he grew older and as circumstances changed. Usually holders of this hypothesis argue that the Apocalypse was written early in eschatological fervor, and that the Gospel is a product of a later, more mature attitude. A major problem with this approach is that the evidence does not allow for a great interval between the composition of each work. There are manuscripts of the Gospel which were copied early in the second century. Further, the Gospel seems to have a complex history of writing and editing. Thus, its early forms at least probably predate the book of Revelation. This theory is not plausible also because it assumes such significant change not only in ideas but also in vocabulary.

The linguistic differences between the Gospel and Revelation have given rise to the theory that a single author, the source of the traditions embodied in the two works, was aided by two different scribes or secretaries. The assumption is that these assistants were given considerable freedom in shaping the two works. This theory explains the differences in syntax and vocabulary, but leaves certain questions unanswered. Paul apparently used secretaries in writing his letters. As far as we know, he used only the one genre. There are significant differences among the Pauline letters, and one can probably speak of development in his thought. But are the differences comparable to those between the Gospel and Revelation? How could two assistants so close to the author have such different perspectives, especially on the question of whether salvation is primarily a matter of the present or the future?

Attempts to overcome the weaknesses of these theories have led to the influential hypothesis that there was a Johannine circle, community, or school. Some scholars use these terms apparently to express the conviction that the literature of the New Testament associated with the name John reflects a type of Christianity different from that reflected in the Synoptic Gospels or in Paul's letters. This conclusion is debatable. It is not obvious that the book of Revelation has more in common with the Gospel of John than it has with 1 Thessalonians or 1 Corinthians.

Other scholars speak of a Johannine school in the technical sense, meaning a group of people engaged in the study of Scripture (what came to be the Old Testament) and in receiving, adapting, and handing on certain forms of Christian tradition. This hypothesis of a Johannine school may be useful in explaining the literary history of the Gospel of John, but it is not of much help in understanding how the Gospel and Revelation are related. The superficial similarities between the two works are best explained as the results of independent adaptations of common traditions. The common traditions do not support the idea of a school, but can be explained more simply as distinct early Christian interpretations of Jewish Scripture and tradition, or as independent adaptations of certain simple and very early Christian traditions, such as the idea of Christ as paschal lamb.

The theory of a Johannine school responsible for both the Gospel and Revelation thus has very little persuasive power. It is clearly not the result of careful historical-critical research, but a prior assumption that shapes the result of the research. The ecclesiastical tradition has bewitched scholars so that they must somehow find a personal, historical, or social relationship between the two books. There is no hard evidence that the Gospel and epistles attributed to John were written in Asia Minor. They could have originated just as well in Syria or Egypt. Bousset was impressed by the fact that the Montanists were inspired, so to speak, by both the Gospel and the Apocalypse. But by their time, the second half of the second century, the association of both works with the name John had occurred already. The Montanists were perhaps under the same spell as many modern scholars. It could be said in response that the reason is more substantial. One could argue that the Gospel reflects a Spirit-inspired form of Christianity in its promise of a Paraclete, and that the prophetic character of Revelation's Spirit-inspired visions is similar. But this similarity is not unique to these two works. The idea of the gift of the Spirit to individual Christians, with its extraordinary consequences, including prophecy, is a common early Christian theme that appears also in Acts and 1 Corinthians.

THE SOCIAL IDENTITY OF THE AUTHOR

Attempts to link the book of Revelation with historical persons, with figures of the early church who are known to us today, have failed. Sound judgment leads to the conclusion that it was written by a man named John who is otherwise unknown to us. A number of recent interpreters of the book have recognized that fact, controlled their curiosity, and wisely given up the search for the historical identity of the author. Some of these have attempted instead to clarify the social identity or social location of the author.

The most fruitful approach to the question of John's social location seems to be to investigate his relationship and the relationship of his book to the phenomenon of early Christian prophecy. Whether or not John was an early Christian prophet and, if he was one, the extent to which he represents the typical phenomenon are matters on which interpreters have disagreed. There is likewise disagreement on whether his book should be described as prophetic, apocalyptic, or both. Various other books of the New Testament refer to early Christian prophets and their activities, the book of Acts and 1 Corinthians being rich in this sort of information. Certain other early Christian texts deal with prophets and prophecy, especially the Didache, that is, *The Teaching of the Twelve Apostles.*

Most scholars who have approached Revelation from this point of view have distinguished community, congregational, or church prophets from wandering prophets. The community prophets are thought of as permanent, settled members of a particular Christian local community or congregation. Wandering prophets in contrast are generally defined as trans-local leaders, who traveled from place to place proclaiming their teaching or the revelations they had received. It is probably wrongheaded to maintain this distinction sharply. Agabus was evidently a member of the congregation in Jerusalem, but occasionally traveled to places like Antioch or Caesarea to deliver a message (Acts 11:27–30 and 21:10–14). Judas and Silas also were apparently members of the community in Jerusalem, but were sent by its leaders with the so-called Apostolic Decree to Antioch, where they exercised their prophetic ministry for a time (Acts 15:22–35). A little later, according to Acts, Silas became Paul's fellow traveler and co-worker (15:40) in Syria, Cilicia, Asia Minor, Macedonia, and Greece.

Silas was apparently the same person referred to as Silvanus by Paul (2 Cor. 1:19; 1 Thess. 1:1). It is important to keep in mind how mobile city dwellers were at that time and the degree to which Christian leadership was trans-local. Thus, any "community prophet" might at some point or for some time behave like a "wandering prophet."

On the other hand, wandering prophets apparently settled down at times and joined particular, local Christian communities. The Didache instructs its readers to share their firstfruits, money, and clothes with any true prophet who wishes to settle among them (13:1). Nevertheless, if not pressed too far, the distinction is probably a useful one; by means of it we can distinguish prophets who at particular times were occupied primarily with local and trans-local ministries, respectively. The distinction is especially important in the light of evidence that at least some wandering prophets had an ascetic life-style. We will return to that question later.

One of the first to discuss the social situation of the book of Revelation was Carl Clemen. In 1927 he published an article arguing that the work represented a small circle of Christians with specific ideas and attitudes that distinguished them from the main body of the church. He apparently came to this conclusion by way of analogy with modern sects.[25] In support of his thesis, he argued that the nature of the symbolism in the book shows that it was written for a small group with specific ideas. He believed that the presentation of the beast, for example, as arising out of the abyss, indicated that what the beast represented was to come in the future. But, he argued, the beast represented Rome, and Rome already existed in the writer's time. He concluded, therefore, that the symbols of Rome were included because the author wanted to present a complete summary of the last things. He was constrained to do so, because of the expectations of his readers. Since—so the argument goes—most Christians would not have held such a complete summary to be indispensable, the book must have been written for a small group.[26] Clemen also argued that the anti-Roman stance of the book reflected a minority opinion.[27]

Clemen's reasoning about the symbolism of the Apocalypse is by no means cogent. It was not unusual for apocalyptic symbols to represent past as well as future events. Consider, for example, the vision of the four beasts coming up out of the sea in Daniel 7. Each of the beasts is related to one of a number of kingdoms, all of which were already in existence at the time the vision was written. Perhaps Clemen intended to say that all apocalyptic symbolism was esoteric and intelligible only to a few. To some degree, apocalypticism was a learned phenomenon. But that does not mean that the apocalypses were intelligible only to a few. The great effort needed to understand them responsibly today is due in large part to the fact that the modern reader must reconstruct the historical situations in which they were written and read, and must recover the connotations of the traditional symbols.

Another aspect of Clemen's intention may have been to point out that the majority of Christians at the time may not have agreed with the book's emphasis on the future and with its anti-Roman stance. Such a judgment may well be correct. But it is quite another matter to conclude that there was an organized, cohesive apocalyptic community to whom the book was addressed. Such a hasty conclusion confuses the question of the author's background and the sources of his ideas with the distinct question of who his audience was. It passes too quickly over the possibility that the author could better be said to have created his audience than to have reflected it. Such a state of affairs could be the result of the author's bringing traditions and a point of view from some other locality to Asia, or to the creative and innovative character of his book, or both.

Nevertheless, Clemen's point of view became quite popular. Günther Bornkamm suggested that the idea of the organization and leadership of the Christian community that is reflected in the book of Revelation was kept alive as late as the time the book was written only by Jewish-Christian conventicles.[28] Like Clemen's language, the word "conventicle" has connotations of the modern sects. Questions immediately arise. Where were such conventicles to be found? What was their origin?

Bornkamm's student Akira Satake pursued these questions. He concluded that the seven congregations mentioned in the Apocalypse, which he saw as seven Jewish-Christian conventicles, were founded by Jewish Christians who migrated from Palestine to Asia Minor in the mid-70s, that is, shortly after the end of the first disastrous Jewish rebellion against Rome. His thesis rests in part on the assumption that the founders of these communities brought with them a community organization which was that of the very earliest Christian community. This organization was one in which the prophets alone were the leaders. Satake assumes that some Jewish Christians maintained this polity in spite of the changes brought about by James, the brother of the Lord, who at an early stage became leader of the congregation in Jerusalem. He also suggests that the author of Revelation came from Palestine. In support of that thesis, he points to John's use of the original Hebrew or Aramaic text of the Bible and to his knowledge of the Apostolic Decree (2:14, 20).[29]

Satake's thesis about the origin of the seven congregations is not persuasive because of its highly speculative character. There is simply not enough positive evidence to support it. In any case, his conceptual framework is faulty, in part because of his assumption that prophets were leaders in an official or institutional sense in the early church. It is also very doubtful that Revelation reflects the actual polity of the seven communities.

A somewhat different approach has been to focus on John's role and to consider its social context. G. Kretschmar suggested that John belonged to a circle of prophets, of which he was possibly the head.[30] Aimo T. Nikolainen also saw John in the social role of prophet and found evidence in Revelation for a group of community prophets in the seven congregations. The book of Revelation opens, "A revelation of Jesus Christ, which God gave him, to show to his servants the things which must happen soon" (1:1). Nikolainen understood these "servants" to be the community prophets who transmitted John's book to the communities, interpreted it for them, and guarded its integrity (see 22:18–19). Since John is also called a "servant" in the opening verse, Nikolainen concluded that John considered himself also to be a community prophet.[31]

In support of this reading of the opening verse, Nikolainen pointed to the account of the vision of a mighty angel in ch. 10. The angel takes an oath that there would be no more delay, but that, when the seventh trumpet is sounded (11:15), the mystery of God would be fulfilled, "as he announced to his servants the prophets" (10:7). In spite of the allusion to Amos 3:7, Nikolainen saw a reference here not to Israelite prophets, but to the Christian community prophets, of whom John was one. He went on to raise the question whether John was simply one of many such prophets, or whether at least he regarded himself as having a special role. In the light of the two passages discussed, Nikolainen concluded that John did distinguish himself from the other prophets as the mediator of the revelation from Christ. His being given the little scroll to eat in ch. 10 shows that his role was analogous to that of the classical prophets of Israel.[32]

Nikolainen cited three other passages which showed, in his opinion, that the community prophets were the only special group singled out from the general body of Christians, the saints, as holding a position of honor and leadership. In 16:6, the plague through which fresh waters are turned to blood is portrayed as divine punishment upon those who shed the blood of "saints and prophets." In 18:20 a call to rejoice over the fall of Babylon is addressed to "heaven and saints and apostles and prophets." Shortly thereafter, it is said that in her (Babylon) was found the blood of prophets and saints and of all who have been slain on earth (18:24).

David Hill has been interested in the same questions as Nikolainen, but has proceeded toward answers somewhat more cautiously. Hill argued that the references to prophets in 10:7, 11:18; 18:20, 24; and 22:6 at least include Christian prophets contemporary with John. He assumed that some of these were settled and active in the seven communities to whom the messages are addressed. He distinguished between the ultimate addressees of the book, the members of the seven congregations, and the persons to whom the book was first delivered.[33] According to 1:1 and 22:6 the book was delivered to the servants of God. Hill pointed out that the phrase "servants of God" in Revelation sometimes means Christians in general (2:20; 7:3; 19:2, 5; and 22:3) and sometimes prophets (10:7 and 11:18). In 11:18 it is not absolutely clear that the words "your servants the prophets" should be taken together as a phrase. The intention may have been to say "your servants, namely prophets and saints and those who fear your name." There is thus only one certain case in which prophets are called God's servants (10:7), which is an allusion to Amos 3:7. The use of the phrase "his servants the prophets" once or even twice does not mean that the word "servants" alone elsewhere in the book refers to prophets.

In 22:16 a saying of Jesus is quoted or prophetically delivered, "I Jesus sent my angel to witness to you [plural] these things for [or about] the congregations." Hill took this remark to mean that the book was delivered to a group who can be differentiated from the ordinary members of the congregations, namely, the community prophets. In support of this conclusion he pointed to a verse earlier in the chapter, "And the Lord, the God of the spirits of the prophets, sent his angel to show his servants what must take place soon" (22:6). He cited three commentators who take "servants" here as a reference to community prophets and affirmed that judgment. The logic seems to be that the juxtaposition of the phrase "the God of the spirits of the prophets" with the phrase "his servants" implies that the servants are the prophets. This is faulty reasoning. The description of the Lord as God of the spirits of the prophets has the effect of emphasizing the divine origin of prophecy and thus serves to enhance the authority of this book. It supports the remark at the beginning of verse 6, "These words are trustworthy and true." It is clear that 22:6 resumes the remarks made in 1:1 about the people for whom the work is intended.

In neither case is there any compelling reason to think that "servants" refers to a special group rather than to the ordinary Christians in the seven congregations.

If "servants" refers to the addressees in general in 22:6, there is little reason to take the "you" of 22:16 as a reference to prophets who receive the revelation "for" the congregations. It is more likely that "you" refers to the ordinary Christians to whom the book is addressed. The second person plural is not so surprising here. It occurs in the messages (2:10, 13, 23, 24, 25), where it is also said that the Spirit speaks to the congregations. The phrase "the Spirit says to the churches," which appears in each message, is analogous to Jesus' sending his angel to the communities and explains how the latter could be said in 22:16. The testimony is thus not given to others "for" the congregations, but to them, and is "about" them.[34]

With regard to the role of John, Hill concluded that he was not typical of the community prophets, if he could be classed among them at all.[35] According to Hill, John was more similar to Jewish prophets than to what we know of early Christian prophets. He presented two arguments in support of this conclusion. One is his perception of a difference in authority between the two types of prophet. The Jewish prophet possessed the Spirit, whereas his addressees did not. The Christian prophet spoke or wrote to brothers and sisters who also thought of themselves as filled with the Spirit. The authority claimed indirectly by John in his book seemed to Hill to be nearly absolute. Hill referred to 1 Cor. 14:29–33 to support his conclusion that a Christian prophet did not stand above the community, but was a member of it and was subject to its judgment.

Now it is interesting to note that Paul did not say that the spirits of the prophets were subject to the community or to the church. Rather, he said that they were subject to the prophets themselves (1 Cor. 14:32). Hill seems to have overstated the subordinate role of the prophets in Corinth. Paul is urging them to conform to the principle of order that he advocates, not to an established community discipline. He exerts his own authority, as an apostle who also has the Spirit, over the prophets. As far as we know, the prophets in Corinth were members of the community who had the gift of prophecy. It is likely that wandering prophets would have had even more independence and authority. The Didache says, "But suffer the prophets to hold Eucharist as they will" (10:7). It seems then that the authority claimed by John may differ in degree from that of some early Christian prophets, but that it was similar in kind.

Hill's other argument for a distinctive role of John is that he mediated revelation to other prophets, who were thus his subordinate assistants, as it were. This argument fails if the book was simply addressed to the members of the seven congregations directly, as 1:4 suggests and as was argued above.

After very persuasively showing the weaknesses of the theory that the author of Revelation belonged to the "Johannine school," Elisabeth Schüssler Fiorenza suggested instead that he was a member of an early Christian prophetic-apocalyptic school. She based this thesis on his familiarity with prophetic-apocalyptic traditions and forms. She went on to argue that he was not only a member of such a school but the head or leader.[36] In support of this second conclusion, she referred to the saying of Jesus in 22:16 regarding his sending his angel to "you" (plural). She interpreted this saying as Hill did, seeing in it a reference to community prophets to whom the book was addressed. Further, she saw an analogy between John and the community prophets, who with him constituted a school, and another group referred to in the message to Thyatira. Schüssler Fiorenza plausibly concluded that the woman described as "Jezebel, who calls herself a prophet" (2:20) was a prophet-teacher whose teaching had persuaded a number of people, namely, "those who commit adultery with her" (2:22). John used such harsh language, according to Schüssler Fiorenza, because he believed that her teaching was harmful. In 2:22 there is a reference to "Jezebel's" children. It is likely, as Schüssler Fiorenza argued, that the term does not refer to her physical offspring, but to her disciples or followers. She went on, however, to argue that this group constituted a school. The hypothetical school of "Jezebel" functions as evidence for the prophetic school headed by John.

In a subsequent article, Schüssler Fiorenza pursued some of the same questions. She argued that the woman called "Jezebel" was a community prophet and the head of a prophetic school, circle, or house church.[37] The influence of this group was felt in Ephesus (the false apostles and the Nicolaitans are seen as part of the same movement; 2:2, 6) and in Pergamum (the teaching of "Balaam" and the Nicolaitans; 2:14, 15), as well as in Thyatira. The false apostles are seen as itinerant, like the wandering prophets, but the others are considered to be settled community prophets who were members of the communities to whom the respective messages are addressed.

In the same article, Schüssler Fiorenza proposed a novel solution to an old, knotty question, namely, why the seven messages are each addressed to the angel of the congregation rather than simply to the congregation itself. The most common interpretation of the angels at present is that they are heavenly beings, the patron angels, in a sense, of the congregations. The source of the idea is generally seen in the Israelite and Jewish apocalyptic notion that each nation has its angelic ruler and heavenly representative. Schüssler Fiorenza's starting point is her interpretation of 22:16, namely, that the book is addressed to community prophets who are expected to mediate it to the ordinary Christians of the seven communities. She found an analogy in the function presupposed for the prophets in that verse and the role of the seven angels in chs. 2 and 3. In spite of the fact that the angels are addressed as if they were the community itself, she assumed that the addressing of the messages to them implied that they were supposed to transmit the messages to the members of the congregation to which they were related. Thus she could see both the prophets and the angels as mediators. She explained the address to angels as a literary convention, used because of the visionary framework. Therefore, she could conclude that the angels are the heavenly counterparts of the community prophets. She used this interpretation of the angels as evidence that John was the leader of a group of prophets who were members of the seven communities, that is, of a prophetic school or circle.[38]

In support of the theory that John led a prophetic school or circle, Schüssler Fiorenza argued that such subordinate prophets would have been necessary to explain the language and imagery of Revelation, since it would not have been accessible to all. She also claimed that John could or would not have written in his own name and under his own prophetic authority if prophecy and prophetic leadership were not significant elements in the lives of the seven congregations.

The first facet of Schüssler Fiorenza's theory that must be examined carefully is the conclusion that John belonged to a prophetic-apocalyptic school or circle. Although they have not yet been studied as thoroughly as they could be, it is clear that John used what might be called prophetic-apocalyptic traditions and forms. But it is doubtful whether this use is sufficient grounds for positing a prophetic-apocalyptic school. The vacillation between the term "school" and the term "circle" reveals either a lack of clear thinking or a scarcity of evidence. She herself has criticized the vacillation in terminology of scholars positing a Johannine school as imprecise. She even quoted B. H. Streeter's telling remark, "The word 'school' is one of those vague, seductive expressions which it is so easy to accept as a substitute for clear thinking."[39]

As Schüssler Fiorenza pointed out, some scholars have attempted to distinguish a school from a sect, circle, community, or tradition by defining a school as a group preoccupied with studying, teaching, learning, and writing. She quoted Krister Stendahl favorably as follows: "Thus the Johannine school method is not what is usually meant by loose citations, or those more or less frequently quoted from memory. It is rather the opposite since the form of John's quotations is certainly the fruit of scholarly treatment of written OT texts."[40] It is doubtful that the book of Revelation can be seen as the product of a school in this technical sense. Whereas the Gospel of John *quotes* the Scripture, Revelation uses the loose form of citation, which Stendahl would exclude from school activity. In fact Revelation does not even cite Scripture, but alludes to it and uses it as raw material in creating a new literary composition.

Schüssler Fiorenza rightly made a strong contrast between early Christian prophecy and early Christian homily and exegesis.[41] She quoted Krister Stendahl with approval once again: "The prophetic spirit creates; it does not quote in order to teach or argue." But are not teaching and arguing essential activities of a school? She went on: "While the homily is the interpretation of the divine word in Scripture, prophecy claims to be the revelation and authority of the Kyrios. ... As the "words of prophecy," [Revelation] does not aim at didactic instruction but at prophetic proclamation." She has assigned to early Christian homily and exegesis the activities typical of a school in the precise sense. It is therefore probably not helpful to speak of a prophetic-apocalyptic school.

Revelation 1:7 is a prophetic saying, "Behold, he is coming with the clouds, and every eye will see him including those who pierced him, and all the tribes of the earth will mourn over him." Schüssler Fiorenza and others have shown that this saying is a product of early Christian exegetical activity. She took the presence of this saying in Revelation as evidence for the association of the book with an early Christian apocalyptic school or tradition.[42] There is, of course, a great difference between an apocalyptic school and a tradition. It is one thing to imagine a group of early Christian apocalyptic prophets handing on tradition and proclaiming their messages in some sort of cooperation. It is quite another to envisage early Christian teachers, homilists, and exegetes studying and handing on various traditions, including some of an apocalyptic nature. The presence of the prophetic saying quoted above is evidence only for the latter, general kind of early Christian learned activity. But Schüssler Fiorenza seems to assume that it is evidence for a distinctly *prophetic* school.

If it does not seem appropriate to conclude that John was a member of a prophetic-apocalyptic *school,* what of the related hypothesis that he belonged to an analogous type of *circle?* Schüssler Fiorenza, as we have seen, argued that the book of Revelation contains evidence for a group of prophets associated with John, who were active in the seven congregations. But there is really very little evidence, if any, that such was the case. We have already seen that the saying in 22:16, "I Jesus sent my angel to witness to you [plural] these things about [or for] the congregations," can be interpreted just as well, if not better, as a reference to the members of the seven communities, rather than to a group of community prophets. If this verse fails to establish such a group, then the interpretation of the seven angels as heavenly counterparts of community prophets loses all persuasive power.

According to Schüssler Fiorenza, a major issue in the seven messages is the rivalry between two opposed prophetic schools, John's and "Jezebel's." It is quite clear that John and the prophet-teacher called Jezebel were competing for the allegiance of Christians at least in Thyatira. It is also likely that "Jezebel" had associates (her "children," 2:23). But it is not necessarily the case that her associates were prophets as she was. The evidence supports speaking of two points of view represented by two persons and their followers, or perhaps of two parties in the region. It does not, however, support the conclusion that there were two rival prophetic *schools.*

Some further questions need to be raised concerning Schüssler Fiorenza's conclusions about the party or movement associated with the woman whom John calls Jezebel. She concluded that the false apostles mentioned in the message to Ephesus belong to the group called Nicolaitans because the angel of the congregation in Ephesus is praised for rejecting both. She infers that two groups with whom John disagreed held the same teaching. This does not necessarily follow. She is right, however, in seeing the Nicolaitans, "Balaam," and "Jezebel" as part of the same movement. The teaching ascribed to all three is the same (2:14, 20). Schüssler Fiorenza assumed that the Nicolaitans got their name from Nicolaus, one of the seven Hellenists mentioned in Acts 6. That was the argument of interpreters of Revelation in the second century and later, but it is not necessarily accurate. Those interpreters may have had no reliable historical information, but drew their conclusion simply by reading Revelation 2 in the light of Acts 6.

Schüssler Fiorenza also concluded that "Jezebel" and the Nicolaitans of Pergamum were settled community prophets. This settled character was in contrast to the situation in Ephesus, where at least the false apostles had a wandering style of life. Now it is clear that the apostles mentioned in the message to Ephesus were itinerant. It is not, however, obvious that the other leaders opposed by John were settled community prophets or teachers. The evidence more easily supports the theory that the leaders called Nicolaitans, "Balaam," and "Jezebel" were itinerant. The fact that several communities were affected by the same teaching supports the theory that the party or movement had a trans-local leadership. It does not follow that all these leaders were prophets. "Jezebel" claimed to be one (2:20) and was apparently recognized by many as such. "Balaam" may have had or claimed a prophetic function, since the allegorical name given him suggests such a role. Although we are not justified in speaking of rival prophetic schools in Asia, we may probably speak of rival prophets.

It is debatable whether the book of Revelation was accessible to all the members of the seven communities or not. Much of the book's power and appeal is due to the fact that many of the images and symbols are not immediately transparent. They do not have a single "correct" meaning or interpretation. The idea that a special, knowledgeable group would have been needed to decode or explain the book underestimates its intrinsic intelligibility and evocative power, especially to people of its own epoch. It is not necessary to be able to identify every allusion to the Jewish Bible to respond to Revelation. The more sensitive or learned members of the community may have aided the less well equipped members in its appreciation. Perhaps teachers were of some help with interpretation. But the theory that a circle of prophets was necessary to make the book accessible is gratuitous.

The fact that John wrote in his own name and claimed to have received divine revelation does not prove that there were community prophets active in one or more of the congregations. The notion that there were people who received divine messages was familiar to anyone who had read or heard of the Israelite prophets or who was familiar with analogous phenomena in the earliest church or elsewhere in the Greco-Roman world. The activity of "Jezebel" and perhaps "Balaam" shows that the phenomenon of prophecy was alive in the region at the time. But there is little if any evidence that John's allies in the seven communities included prophets. The references to prophets discussed by Nikolainen and Hill (10:7; 11:18; 16:6; 18:20, 24; and 22:6) could be interpreted entirely in terms of the classical Israelite prophets. After all, early Christians believed that they had prophesied the events of Christ's life and work and the other last things. It was assumed by early Christians that many, if not all, of the classical prophets had been martyred; see, for example, Matt. 5:12; 23:29–39; Luke 11:47–51; Acts 7:51–53. Finally, John did not distinguish between the Jewish people and the Christian church, between old and new covenant. This becomes especially clear in ch. 12.[43] Thus he could treat the classical prophets as part of the one true Israel. But even if these passages include Christian as well as Jewish prophets as Hill argued, it does not mean that any of these were active in John's time in any of the seven congregations. As Ulrich Müller has well pointed out, the references are very general.[44]

The social location of John, author of Revelation, was taken up in a recent article by David Aune. He noted that John never referred to himself as a "prophet," but implied that he played that role by describing his book as a "prophecy" (1:3; 22:7, 10, 18, 19). Further, John came very close to designating himself a prophet when he attributed the following words to the revealing angel in 22:9: "I am your fellow servant, and the fellow servant of your brothers the prophets." Aune interpreted this remark as evidence that John was a member of a prophetic circle or guild. He found support for that conclusion, as did Hill and Schüssler Fiorenza, in 22:16 ("I Jesus sent my angel to witness to you [plural] these things about [or for] the congregations"). He concluded that John, like "Jezebel," belonged to an association of prophets found in many if not most of the seven congregations.[45]

Aune criticized the modern distinction between itinerant prophets, who reflected an early Christian Palestinian tradition, and community prophets, who reflected Hellenistic tradition, as an oversimplification. He emphasized the highly mobile way of life in Greco-Roman society at the time and suggested that early Christians followed older Jewish patterns of travel and communication. He argued that there were at least three types of early Christian itinerant prophets:

(1) the prophet who traveled to a particular place to execute a divine commission (Acts, Shepherd of Hermas), (2) the prophet who traveled a circuit with some regularity (John the prophet), and (3) prophets whose wandering was an enactment of the ascetic values of homelessness, lack of family ties and the rejection of wealth and possessions (Peregrinus, prophets of the Didache, and prophets of the Q-Community).[46]

Even though John did not designate himself as a prophet, it is likely that he considered his function to be a prophetic one, and that he made an indirect claim to be a true prophet in contrast to the false prophets "Jezebel" and "Balaam." But Aune's interpretation of 22:9 is problematic. The phrase "your brothers the prophets" does not compel the conclusion that John was a member of a prophetic circle or guild in any local sense. It is, like other references to prophets in Revelation, a very general one. It could be understood perfectly well as an allusion to the classical prophets of Israel. The angel's remark would then have the function of impressing upon the readers that God was then speaking through John as God formerly spoke through the prophets of old. Even if the phrase includes Christian prophets, there is no persuasive reason to think of prophets associated with the seven communities. The saying in 22:16, as we have seen, does not support Aune's view in any cogent way.

As noted earlier, the contrast between itinerant or wandering prophets and settled or community prophets cannot be held rigidly. Aune is quite right in distinguishing various motivations for traveling about. His types (1) and (3) are characterized by different motivations, whereas type (2), the category to which he assigns John, is not. If John did confine his travels to the seven congregations, a conclusion of which we can by no means be certain, his motivation may have been either the execution of a divine commission or the enactment of ascetic values, or both. Although the ascetic form of wandering may have its roots in Palestine, there is no reason to limit it to that region. If the practice could spread to Syria, it could have spread farther. There is a remarkable analogy between the ascetic values of Aune's third type and the message of the Apocalypse. We will return to this topic in Chapter 4, "Social Radicalism in the Apocalypse."

What then can be said about the social location of John, author of the book of Revelation? He apparently claimed (indirectly) to be, and was recognized by at least some as, an early Christian prophet. He does not seem to have distinguished Christian from Israelite prophets, and his self-understanding and self-presentation were shaped by the records and traditions of the classical prophets. The evidence suggests that John was an itinerant prophet who was familiar with all seven communities because he had visited and worked with each of them. If one of the towns served as his primary residence, we have no reliable way of determining which of them it was.[47] The frequently advocated thesis that he was a member or the head of a prophetic school or local circle of prophets is without foundation.

It has often been assumed or argued that John was a native Palestinian and a Jew by birth. He was apparently not a Judaizer; that is, he did not insist that all followers of Christ be circumcised and observe the Sabbath and other cultic regulations of the law. He condemned "harlotry," which probably meant idolatry, and eating meat sacrificed to idols. These requirements were a minimal standard for Gentile Christians, similar to the so-called Apostolic Decree (Acts 15). Such a stance is certainly compatible with Jewish birth, as we know from Paul's letters and Acts.

Although the possibility that John was born a Gentile cannot be excluded, it is likely that he was a Jew by birth. Such a hypothesis helps explain his massive assumption of continuity; that is, his failure to distinguish an old and a new Israel. He had, to be sure, his enemies among the Jewish people, but he claims (indirectly) the designation "Jew" for the followers of Jesus (2:9; 3:9). It also makes John's thorough and deep knowledge of the Jewish Bible understandable, as well as the similarities in form and content between his book and the Jewish apocalypses. Finally, his fierce anti-Roman stance shows that he was heir to certain strands of Jewish tradition, as we shall see.

It is also likely that John was a native of Palestine, or lived there for an extended period. Many people in the eastern Mediterranean region in John's time were bilingual or trilingual. Thus language is not a sure guide to native origin. Nevertheless, it is unlikely that a Jew of the Diaspora would have known Hebrew or Aramaic, unless he had lived and studied for a considerable time in Palestine. It is probable that John knew two or three languages. Besides Greek, he seems to have known Mishnaic Hebrew (the Hebrew of his day) or Aramaic, or both. It has long been noted that John's Greek is very peculiar. In fact he made many gross errors in grammar and syntax. Dionysius of Alexandria was the first, as far as we know, to point out this feature. R. H. Charles attributed it to the (hypothetical) fact that he had learned Greek at an advanced age and therefore imperfectly. G. Mussies made some striking observations in a recent article. He noted that John avoided typically Greek syntactical constructions that had no counterpart in Hebrew or Aramaic. Not only that, but in one type of case he avoided a construction that had a counterpart in biblical Hebrew, but none in Mishnaic Hebrew and Galilean Aramaic.[48] Although there are many Semitisms in Revelation, the ones typical of the Septuagint are avoided.[49]

It is hard to avoid the conclusion that John was at least bilingual. But why was his mastery of Greek so imperfect? Charles's theory is not persuasive. If a man of John's creative intelligence was unable to master Greek because of personal circumstances, one would expect him to have sought and received assistance. It is more likely that John wrote a peculiar, contemporarily Semitizing Greek on purpose. Such an act may have been a kind of protest against the higher forms of Hellenistic culture. It would have been an act of cultural pride of a Jewish Semite. Such an act fits well with the type of message expressed in Revelation, as we shall see. It is analogous to the refusal of some American blacks to "talk right."

Satake argued, following Charles, that John was a Palestinian because of his use of the original Hebrew or Aramaic text of the Jewish Bible. Charles's conclusion, however, is no longer tenable. First of all, recent scholarship has emphasized that John did not quote the Bible. Charles was aware of that fact, but assumed that John incorporated phrases and clauses from it, which he copied word for word, either from the original text or a Greek version. More recent scholars have understood John's procedure as an allusive, "anthological" style, in which the words, images, phrases, and patterns of the Bible are raw material for a new literary creation and prophetic proclamation.[50] In such a style, one cannot be sure of finding phrases and clauses that translate exactly the text or reproduce precisely the version with which John was familiar. He may have relied on his memory, which may not always have been accurate. Or, more likely, he may have altered the wording deliberately in order to create the desired effect.

Another factor in the question of what form of the Bible John used is the complex history of the Hebrew and Aramaic text and of the Greek version. Charles divided John's allusions to the Bible into three groups: (1) passages based directly on the Hebrew of the Old Testament (or the Aramaic in parts of Daniel); (2) passages based on the Hebrew or Aramaic, but influenced by the Septuagint; (3) passages based on the Hebrew or Aramaic, but influenced by a later form of the Septuagint, such as is preserved in Theodotion.[51] These categories need to be revised in light of recent discoveries and research. Theodotion, according to the tradition of the early church, translated the Jewish Bible into Greek in the second century C.E.[52] Since sometimes John's allusions are closer to Theodotion's readings than to the Septuagint's, Charles inferred, as had others, that a forerunner of Theodotion's version existed in John's time. In 1953 D. Barthélemy published fragments of a previously unknown recension of the Greek Bible, fragments discovered in a cave beside one of the wadis that empty into the Dead Sea. The parts of the recension actually discovered are from the twelve Minor Prophets. But Barthélemy showed that the recension existed in many other books of the Bible, including Daniel. Barthélemy named this recension the *kaige* recension, because of a Greek word that appears frequently in it. It has been dated to the second half of the first century C.E., early enough for John to have known it. It is a revision of the Old Greek (Septuagint) text, based on a forerunner of the Masoretic text extant in Palestine toward the middle of the first century C.E.[53]

The *kaige* recension sought to bring the Greek version into line with a new form of the Hebrew text, an ancestor of the Masoretic text which Charles had compared with John's allusions. The existence of this recension undercuts Charles's theory that John used the original Hebrew or Aramaic text. It raises the possibility that the deviations from the Septuagint reflect the *kaige* recension and not the Hebrew or Aramaic text.

Another reason for linking John with Palestine is the similarity between his work and the fourth book of the *Sibylline Oracles*. *Sib. Or.* 4 is a Jewish work that is modeled on pagan sibylline oracles for apologetic purposes, in part. It is dated to about 80 C.E. Some scholars have argued that it was composed in Asia Minor because of an oracle concerning Asia in lines 145–148. But *Sib. Or.* 5 has a similar oracle (350–355) and is clearly of Egyptian origin. It is more likely that *Sib. Or.* 4 was composed in the Jordan valley, or perhaps in Syria, because of its marked interest in baptism.[54]

Sib. Or. 4 and Revelation belong to the same literary category, revelatory literature. There are similarities in content as well. Both works are anti-Roman and have a strong interest in the last things. The legend of Nero's flight to the Parthians and his future return not only is reflected in each work but is a significant theme in both. Both compositions reject the idea of a physical, earthly temple. Ultimate salvation in both works involves the raising of the good from death to life on a new earth.

If John did bring sibylline traditions from Palestine to Asia Minor, he probably was not bringing something utterly unknown or new to the region. *Sib. Or.* 1–2 is a Christian redaction of an older, Jewish work. The Jewish substratum probably was written in Phrygia no later than the time of Augustus. It showed considerable interest in the last things and apparently envisaged the dominion of the Hebrews in a final earthly kingdom. It also looked forward to the resurrection of the dead, the punishment of the wicked by fire, and the transformation of the earth.[55]

CONCLUSION

Although we must admit that we cannot identify the author of Revelation with any historical person otherwise known, we can infer a great deal about his social identity. He played the role of prophet; that is, his function was to mediate an intelligible message to his fellow Christians, a message that he claimed derived ultimately from God. He was clearly influenced by the written records and oral traditions about the classical prophets of Israel, but at the same time he should be seen as part of the phenomenon of early Christian prophecy. Early Christian prophecy was evidently very widespread in Paul's time. Whereas the function had diminished or even died out in some communities, it was still alive in the province of Asia, as the activities of

"Jezebel" and "Balaam" show, alongside John's own. John was probably a Jew by birth and either was a native of Palestine or lived there for an extended period. He knew one or more Semitic languages, as well as Greek. Two aspects of his social identity are very important for understanding the origin and meaning of his book. One is his affinity with the Jewish sibylline tradition. The other is his role as an itinerant prophet. These aspects will be discussed in Chapters 3 and 4.

Now that we know something of the author, we must ask when his book was written. Since Revelation is so greatly oriented toward social and political matters, it is absolutely essential that it be dated as precisely as possible. Otherwise, the allusions to its situation might be seriously misinterpreted and its purpose misunderstood.

NOTES

1. Edgar Goodspeed and Robert M. Grant, *A History of Early Christian Literature* (University of Chicago Press, 1966), pp. 90–91.

2. Ibid., p. 91; Henry B. Swete, *The Apocalypse of St. John*, 3d ed. (London: Macmillan & Co., 1909), p. cviii.

3. See the anecdote related by Martin Kähler and quoted by Van Harvey, *The Historian and the Believer* (Macmillan Co., 1966; repr. Westminster Press, 1981), pp. 102–103.

4. Werner G. Kümmel, *Introduction to the New Testament*, 14th rev. ed. (Abingdon Press, 1966), p. 170.

5. R. H. Charles, *A Critical and Exegetical Commentary on the Revelation of St. John*, ICC (Charles Scribner's Sons, 1920), Vol. 1, pp. xlv–xlix.

6. Swete, *The Apocalypse of St. John*, p. clxxv.

7. Ibid., p. cxi.

8. Eusebius, *Hist. Eccl.* 3.28.

9. Jean Daniélou and Henri Marrou, *The First Six Hundred Years* (McGraw-Hill Book Co., 1964), p. 59.

10. Kümmel, *Introduction to the New Testament*, p. 350.

11. Dionysius is quoted by Eusebius, *Hist. Eccl.* 7.25.

12. Kümmel, *Introduction to the New Testament,* p. 330.

13. Stephen Neill, *The Interpretation of the New Testament 1861–1961* (Oxford University Press, 1964), pp. 19–28; Elisabeth Schüssler Fiorenza, "The Quest for the Johannine School: The Apocalypse and the Fourth Gospel," *NTS* 23 (1976–77), p. 403.

14. Kümmel, *Introduction to the New Testament,* p. 331.

15. G. B. Caird, *A Commentary on the Revelation of St. John the Divine* (Harper & Row, 1966), p. 4; Charles, *A Critical and Exegetical Commentary on the Revelation of St. John,* Vol. 1, pp. xlix–l.

16. See the story about the Gospel of Peter recorded by Eusebius, *Hist. Eccl.* 6.12.

17. Goodspeed and Grant, *A History of Early Christian Literature,* p. 91; see 1 Peter 5:13.

18. Henry Chadwick, *The Early Church* (Penguin Books, 1967), p. 64.

19. Eusebius, *Hist. Eccl.* 7.25.

20. Ibid., 3.39; the translation used is that in Kümmel, *Introduction to the New Testament,* p. 171.

21. Swete, *The Apocalypse of St. John,* p. clxxvii.

22. Kümmel, *Introduction to the New Testament,* p. 331.

23. J. Massyngberde Ford, *Revelation,* AB (Doubleday & Co., 1975), pp. 3–4.

24. Schüssler Fiorenza, "The Quest for the Johannine School," pp. 410–411.

25. Carl Clemen, "Die Stellung der Offenbarung Johannis im ältesten Christentum," *ZNW* 26 (1927), p. 186.

26. Ibid., pp. 180–181.

27. Ibid., p. 186.

28. Bornkamm is quoted by Ulrich B. Müller, *Zur frühchristlichen Theologiegeschichte* (Gütersloh: Gütersloher Verlagshaus Gerd Mohn, 1976), p. 29.

29. Akira Satake, *Die Gemeindeordnung in der Johannesapokalypse* (Neukirchen-Vluyn: Neukirchener Verlag, 1966), esp. pp. 191–193.

30. G. Kretschmar is cited by Müller, *Zur frühchristlichen Theologie-geschichte,* p. 34.

31. Aimo T. Nikolainen, "Über die theologische Eigenart der Offenbarung des Johannes," *TLZ* 93 (1968), p. 162.

32. Ibid., pp. 162–163.

33. David Hill, "Prophecy and Prophets in the Revelation of St. John," *NTS* 18 (1971–72), pp. 412–413.

34. *Epi* with the dative case at times means "about"; see Walter Bauer, *A Greek-English Lexicon of the New Testament and Other Early Christian Literature,* ed. by W. F. Arndt, F. W. Gingrich, and F. W. Danker, 2d ed. (University of Chicago Press, 1979), p. 287.

35. Hill, "Prophecy and Prophets in the Revelation of St. John," p. 415.

36. Schüssler Fiorenza, "The Quest for the Johannine School," pp. 424–425.

37. Elisabeth Schüssler Fiorenza, "Apokalypsis and Propheteia: The Book of Revelation in the Context of Early Christian Prophecy," in J. Lambrecht (ed.), *L'Apocalypse johannique et l'apocalyptique dans le Nouveau Testament* (Gembloux: J. Duculot, 1980), p. 119.

38. Ibid., pp. 120–121, 127.

39. Schüssler Fiorenza, "The Quest for the Johannine School," p. 407.

40. Ibid.

41. Schüssler Fiorenza, "Apokalypsis and Propheteia," p. 109.

42. Schüssler Fiorenza, "The Quest for the Johannine School," pp. 420–421.

43. The woman in the narrative of ch. 12 represents the heavenly Israel; she is both the Israel from whom the Messiah came according to the flesh and the Israel who was being persecuted for belief in the Messiah. In our language, she is both the Old and the New Israel.

44. Müller, *Zur frühchristlichen Theologiegeschichte,* pp. 31–32.

45. David Aune, "The Social Matrix of the Apocalypse of John," *BR* 26 (1981), pp. 18–19, 29.

46. Ibid., p. 27.

47. Aune argued that Ephesus was John's primary residence (ibid., pp. 27–28) because his opposition to the Nicolaitans was apparently successful there. But he has things to criticize about the Ephesians, whereas he has no censure for the Smyrnaeans or the Philadelphians. The argument based on success in Ephesus is not compelling.

48. G. Mussies, "The Greek of the Book of Revelation," in Lambrecht (ed.), *L'Apocalypse johannique et l'apocalyptique dans le Nouveau Testament,* pp. 167–168.

49. Ibid., pp. 170–171.

50. Schüssler Fiorenza, "Apokalypsis and Propheteia," pp. 108–109.

51. Charles, *A Critical and Exegetical Commentary on the Revelation of St. John,* Vol. 1, pp. lxvi–lxxxi.

52. John W. Wevers, "Theodotion," *IDB* (1962), Vol. 4, pp. 618–619.

53. Frank Moore Cross, Jr., *The Ancient Library of Qumran,* pp. 27–28; Kevin G. O'Connell, "Greek Versions (Minor)," IDBSup (1976), pp. 377–381; Robert A. Kraft, "Septuagint: B. Earliest Greek Versions ('Old Greek')," IDBSup (1976), pp. 811–815.

54. John J. Collins, Introduction to *The Sibylline Oracles,* Book 4, in J. H. Charlesworth (ed.), *Old Testament Pseudepigrapha* (Doubleday & Co., 1983), p. 382.

55. Ibid., Introduction to *The Sibylline Oracles,* Books 1 and 2.

2

When Was Revelation Written?

The conclusions reached in Chapter 1 about the social identity of John the prophet, author of the book of Revelation, provide us with some valuable points of orientation in seeking to place the book in its historical context and to understand it both as a product of its time and as a response to and shaper of its environment. The purpose of this chapter is to determine as precisely as possible the date when Revelation was written. Knowledge of the date of composition can help in deciding how and why the author shaped his raw materials into a new and distinctive composition. To what events was he responding? What factors in the historical and social situation did he consider significant? When the date has been fixed as nearly as possible, the interpreter can discern historical events and social realities reflected in the book's images and narratives. We are then better able to assess the author's purpose in writing the book and its function for the earliest readers.

By speaking of a single date, I express my conviction that the book was given something very close to its present form by a single author at a particular time. He certainly drew upon tradition; probably in a few passages he made use of written sources. But the unity of style and the complex but careful and deliberate design of the book as a whole make hypotheses about the compilation of extensive written sources or a series of editions superfluous.

EXTERNAL EVIDENCE FOR THE DATE

Determining the date of Revelation is a complex task for which there is evidence of different kinds and of varying weight. One type of evidence is external to the book itself, namely, the testimony of other early Christian writers. The earliest witness is Irenaeus, who says that the Apocalypse was seen at the end of the reign of Domitian.[1] Since Domitian ruled from 81 to 96, Irenaeus' comment refers to 95 or 96. The wording leaves open the possibility that Irenaeus believed the book to have been written down somewhat later, especially since he says elsewhere that John lived in Ephesus until the time of Trajan. Trajan was emperor from 98 to 117. But we cannot put much weight on the latter remark, since, as we saw in Chapter 1, Irenaeus is not reliable on figures of the first century. His remark about John living until the reign of Trajan could be due to his confusion of John the prophet with another John or to the development of a legend about John the apostle.

Victorinus, who lived in Pettau (modern Austria), died in 303 in the persecution of Diocletian. He wrote a commentary in Latin on Revelation that is the earliest surviving full commentary on the book.[2] Victorinus and Eusebius say that Revelation was written during the reign of Domitian. They add that John was banished to Patmos by Domitian and that he was released when Domitian died.[3] Commentators have disagreed about whether this tradition of John's banishment is reliable historical information or a legendary motif inspired by Rev. 1:9, "I John . . . was on the island which is called Patmos on account of the word of God and the testimony of Jesus." Some have argued that John was not banished to Patmos but went there voluntarily either to proclaim his teaching or to prepare for a revelatory experience. These two theories must be excluded on linguistic grounds. In the book of Revelation the preposition translated "on account of" never has the sense "for the purpose of," but always gives the grounds, the *past* reason for something. Even though Irenaeus does not mention John's banishment, it is likely that Victorinus and Eusebius have preserved accurate and valuable information on this point. If John was indeed banished, that fact tells us a great deal about the attitude of the Roman authorities toward him and his message and about his own probable attitude toward them. We will pursue this question in Chapter 3.

A few late sources date Revelation to the time of Claudius, Nero, or Trajan. These texts show that there were traditions about the date that were apparently independent of Irenaeus. Their historical reliability, however, is doubtful.[4] The date in Trajan's reign may be based on Irenaeus' remark that John lived to that time. The dates in the reigns of Claudius and Nero may be due to erroneous inferences from the text itself. A date in either of their reigns is excluded for various reasons, as we shall see.

Irenaeus' testimony has been questioned recently on the grounds that he believed both Revelation and the Fourth Gospel to have been written by the apostle John.[5] If Irenaeus was wrong about authorship, so the argument goes, he may have been wrong about the date too. As we noted in Chapter 1, if the apostle John survived until the end of the reign of Domitian, he must have been an extremely old man at that time. The fact that Irenaeus dated the book as he did, in spite of the difficulty about the apostle's age, suggests that he had independent and strong evidence for the date.

Another objection to Irenaeus' dating could be raised on the basis of Domitian's portrayal as the second persecutor, a new Nero, in Christian tradition. There is extremely little evidence that this tradition was accurate. The earliest explicit evidence for it is a passage from a lost book by Melito, who was bishop of Sardis in about 160–170. Melito's book was an apology for Christianity dedicated to the emperor Marcus Aurelius. It was called *To Antoninus* and was quoted by Eusebius.[6] Melito's presentation of the attitudes of the emperors toward Christians is not very accurate. It appears that he wanted to show that only those emperors who had a bad reputation among Romans themselves persecuted Christians, not because Christians deserved punishment, but because those emperors were evil. Nero had indeed instigated violence against Christians in Rome. Domitian was called a second Nero by some writers, so that it would have been easy for Melito to assimilate the later to the earlier.[7] Once the assimilation was made, it seems, it became traditional. Details were added and particular names associated with Domitian's alleged persecution.[8] An objection, therefore, could be made to Irenaeus' dating by raising the possibility that he was unduly influenced by Melito or that he reasoned in the same way as Melito. One might argue that Irenaeus, knowing that Revelation was not written under Nero or judging on the basis of the book itself that it could not have been, concluded that it must have been written under Domitian in response to the persecution he authorized.

This line of argumentation is not persuasive. Irenaeus' reason for dating Revelation to the reign of Domitian does not seem to be the tradition that Domitian was the second great persecutor of Christians. He does not mention any persecution in connection with the book or with the emperor. He does not even mention John's exile to Patmos. If Irenaeus knew the tradition that Domitian was a second Nero, he shows no interest in it. It is likely that he had another reason for dating the book as he did, perhaps information he received from other Christians of Asia Minor.

INTERNAL EVIDENCE FOR THE DATE

Irenaeus' testimony is crucial because the later writers who date Revelation to Domitian's reign could be dependent on him. There seems to be no good reason for doubting Irenaeus' date on grounds external to the book. His dating can be accepted, however, only if it is harmonious with the evidence found within the book itself.

THE NAME BABYLON

The book of Revelation announces and describes in several places the destruction of a city called Babylon (14:8; 16:19; 17:5; 18:2, 10, 21). It is highly unlikely that John would have been so interested in the fall of the historical Babylon, whether the major one in the sixth century B.C.E. or one of the minor ones in the Hellenistic period.[9] It is equally improbable that John hoped for the destruction of the fortified town called Babylon at the head of the Nile delta in Egypt.[10] The reader is given a clear hint that the name is not to be taken literally. In ch. 17 the city is seen in a vision as a woman. In the woman's description it is said, "and upon her forehead a name was written, a mystery, Babylon the great, the mother of prostitutes and of the abominations of the earth" (17:5). The use of the word "mystery" implies that the name Babylon obscures as much as it reveals. Later the mystery is explained, when the interpreting angel tells the seer, "I will tell you the mystery of the woman and of the beast which carries her, which has the seven heads and the ten horns" (17:7). Two remarks in the angel's explanatory speech make clear that the woman represents the city of Rome: "the seven heads are seven mountains upon which the woman sits" (v. 9) and "the woman whom you saw is the great city which holds rule over the kings of the earth" (v. 18). Rome as "the city of the seven hills" was a common expression in classical writers.[11] Likewise, the dominant city of the Mediterranean world in John's time was obviously Rome.

Most commentators agree that "Babylon" in the Apocalypse is a symbolic name for Rome. It is important to recognize that Babylon was not the obvious or only name that a Christian familiar with Jewish tradition might select as a symbolic name for Rome, to portray the city as the enemy of God's people. "Egypt," "Kittim," and "Edom" appear along with "Babylon" in Jewish sources as symbolic names for Rome. In fact, "Edom" is the most common in the rabbinic literature.[12] Most of the occurrences of Babylon as a symbolic name for Rome in Jewish literature are in the Apocalypse of Ezra (4 Ezra

= 2 Esdras 3–14), the Syriac Apocalypse of Baruch (2 *Apoc. Bar.*),
and the fifth book of the *Sibylline Oracles.* In each case where it occurs
in these three works, the context makes it abundantly clear why the
name Babylon was chosen.[13] Rome is called Babylon because her
forces, like those of Babylon at an earlier time, destroyed the temple
and Jerusalem. It is probable that John learned this symbolic name
from his fellow Jews and that it quickly became traditional.

The majority of interpreters have overlooked the importance of
this symbolic name for the date. They have seen it only as a symbol
of great power, wealth, or decadence and have missed its allusion to
the events of 70 C.E. The use of the name is a weighty internal
indication of the date. It is highly unlikely that the name would have
been used before the destruction of the temple by Titus. This internal
evidence thus points decisively to a date after 70 C.E.

THE SEVEN KINGS

The speech of the interpreting angel in ch. 17 contains another
passage that, at first sight, seems to offer important evidence for the
date of Revelation. After remarking that the seven heads of the beast
are seven mountains, the angel continues: "And they are seven kings;
five have fallen, one is, the other has not yet come, and when he comes,
he must remain a little while. And the beast which was and is not, he
himself is also an eighth and is one of the seven, and he goes to
destruction" (vs. 9–11). It would appear that the Apocalypse was
composed under the ruler referred to in the remark, "one is," and that
the interpreter need only calculate who that ruler was to discover the
date of composition. Few interpreters have found that calculation an
easy matter!

First of all, it is necessary to understand the symbol of the beast.
Hermann Gunkel, in a masterful study near the end of the nineteenth
century, showed that the beast is a traditional motif that has its roots
in ancient Near Eastern myths.[14] The implication is that the beast in
Revelation is not a simple historical allegory or an original metaphor.
It may well have allegorical and metaphorical characteristics, but it
carries with it a rich heritage of connotations that derive from the
functions of the creation and combat myths in which it traditionally
appears. Thus the beast evokes a sense of rebellion, chaos, and sterility, qualities associated with the mythic monsters who rebelled against
the creator or hero god in the myths. On one level of meaning, the
beast represents the Roman Empire, but this allegorical function does
not exhaust the meaning of the symbol.

A comparison of the attributes and especially the functions of the beasts mentioned in 11:7; 13:1–10; and ch. 17 shows that they are equivalent in meaning. Like the four beasts of Daniel 7, the beast of Revelation 13 and 17 sometimes represents a kingdom (the Roman Empire) and sometimes a king (the Emperor Nero). It is clear that the legend of Nero's return is reflected in Revelation 13 and 17. Shortly after Nero committed suicide in 68, the rumor began to spread that he had not really died, but had escaped to the East. The common people in Rome and many in the East whom he had benefited hoped that he would return with the Parthians (successors of the Persians) as his allies and regain power in Rome. The Jewish author of the fourth book of the *Sibylline Oracles* adapted this legend in a way that was both anti-Nero and anti-Roman. Several oracles in *Sib. Or.* 3 and 5 make use of the Nero legend so that Nero is portrayed as the adversary of God in the final struggle of the last days. These oracles were written in Egypt between 70 and 130 C.E. John adapted the legend, so that Nero is depicted as an Antichrist. He fits that role exactly, although the name is not used. In Revelation, Nero is an opposing parody of the Lamb, a dying and rising destroyer, rather than savior.[15]

In Rev. 13:3 it is said that one of the heads of the beast had a mortal wound. This is a reference to Nero and his violent death. It is clear, therefore, that one of the seven heads which are kings in ch. 17 is the historical Nero. The beast who will return as the "eighth" is Nero returned from death to life, the Antichrist. It follows that Revelation must have been written after the death of Nero, after 68, because the parallel between him and Jesus requires such a conclusion.

The identity of the other heads is difficult to determine. There are four basic positions on the issue. (1) The seven heads included all the Roman emperors who had ruled up to the author's time, starting at the beginning and counting consecutively. Revelation was thus written under the sixth emperor. Some who take this position begin with Julius Caesar, others with Augustus. Some include the emperors who each ruled for a short time after Nero's death, Galba, Otho, and Vitellius; others omit them.[16] (2) This position is the same as the first, except that the author is not actually writing under the sixth emperor. Some hold *(a)* that an earlier source was used and not updated;[17] others hold *(b)* that an earlier source was used and reinterpreted;[18] and others *(c)* that the author antedated his work; that is, he purposely gave the impression that he was writing under the sixth emperor, when in fact he wrote at a later date.[19] (3) The seven heads do not represent all the Roman emperors, but only selected ones.[20] Sev-

eral different theories about the principle of selection have been proposed. (4) The seven kings are not seven specific, historical kings, but
are purely symbolic.[21]

The theory that the seven heads are intended to include all the
Roman emperors who reigned up to the writer's time has little to
recommend it. It is based on an analogy with Suetonius' *The Twelve
Caesars*, the list of rulers in *Sib. Or.* 5:12–51, and the eagle vision of
4 Ezra 11–12. Suetonius' work belongs to a quite different genre. The
interest in completeness and consecutive order is explicit. The sibylline oracle also has a different literary form and interest. It begins by
calling itself the chronicle of the sons of Latium. A chronicle by
definition must relate events in chronological order and be relatively
complete.

The comparison of Revelation 17 with the eagle vision of 4 Ezra
is very instructive. The eagle is described as having twelve wings, eight
little opposing wings, and three heads. The twelve wings clearly represent Roman emperors, beginning with Julius Caesar, since the second
is unmistakably Augustus (2 Esdr. 11:13–17; 12:14–15). The identity
of the little opposing wings is very hard to establish.[22] If the vision has
any interest in completeness, it is expressed in these two series of
wings. The heads, on the other hand, represent three emperors selected from the total list. The description of the heads indicates that
they stand for Vespasian and his two sons, Titus and Domitian. It is
quite clear then that these three emperors are represented both by
three of the twelve major wings and by the three heads.

Revelation 17 and 4 Ezra 11–12 are certainly of the same literary
form. The use of imagery in the eagle vision, however, does not
support the assumption that all the seven heads of Revelation 17
represent all the emperors up to the actual or fictitious time of writing.
If there is an analogy, the ten horns of Revelation 17 might correspond to the twelve wings and represent all the emperors, whereas the
seven heads would correspond to the three heads of the eagle and
represent a selection. But the ten horns more likely refer to Nero's
Parthian allies.[23] In any case, the similarity between the two vision
accounts should not be pressed, and we cannot assume that John was
following the example of 4 Ezra or that he used traditional images in
exactly the same way.

A further problem with the theory that the seven heads represent
all the emperors is that, if one begins counting with Julius Caesar,
Nero is the sixth. Since Nero's death is presupposed in the imagery,
he cannot be the "one [who] is." Holders of this position who recognize this problem solve it by beginning with Augustus rather than

Caesar. To justify this some point to Tacitus, saying that he regarded the empire as beginning with Augustus. In *Hist.* 1.1 Tacitus says:

> I shall begin my work with the year [69 C.E.] in which Servius Galba and Titus Vinius were consuls, the former for the second time. My choice of starting point is determined by the fact that the preceding period of 820 years dating from the foundation of Rome has found many historians. So long as republican history was their theme, they wrote with equal eloquence of style and independence of outlook. But when the battle of Actium had been fought and the interests of peace demanded the concentration of power in the hands of one man, this great line of classical historians came to an end.[24]

Tacitus is making a critical judgment about Roman historians and not defining the beginning of the empire as such. He does not mention Julius Caesar and one can conclude at most that he was a borderline figure. Tacitus' failure to mention him in this context may be due simply to the fact that his rule was too short to be of significance for the practical matter Tacitus is discussing. Furthermore, Tacitus does not begin his own history with Augustus, but with Galba.

The opening passage of the *Annals* also does not support the theory that Tacitus considered Julius Caesar to belong to the republic and the empire to begin only with Augustus:

> Neither Cinna nor Sulla created a lasting despotism: Pompey and Crassus quickly forfeited their power to Caesar, and Lepidus and Antony their swords to Augustus, who, under the style of "Prince" [*princeps*], gathered beneath his empire a world outworn by civil broils.[25]

Their titles were certainly different, but Tacitus seems to be drawing a parallel between the two in this passage. A. A. Bell argued that "Tacitus clearly considers the assumption of this title *princeps* to be the major distinction between the emperors and all the earlier magistrates of the Roman state. Julius never held that title, and throughout his work Tacitus pointedly differentiates *dictatorem Caesarem aut imperatorem Augustum.*"[26] But the passages he cites do not support this conclusion. Yes, Tacitus distinguishes their *titles,* but not their *functions.* In *Ann.* 4.34 the deified Julius and the deified Augustus are called "the Caesars," and in 13:3 both are included in a list of masters of the empire.

In any case, it is more likely that John was influenced by Jewish writers than by Roman. The sibylline chronicle (*Sib. Or.* 5:12–51) and the eagle vision of 4 Ezra both begin with Julius Caesar. Josephus also apparently considered the empire to begin with Julius Caesar. In *Ant.* 18.32 he refers to Augustus as "the second emperor (*autokratōr)* of the Romans." If the theory that the seven heads represent all emperors in succession leads to an impossibility (that Revelation was written under Nero), one should seek another interpretative principle rather than make a weakly justified modification in the theory.

The theory that the seven heads represent all the emperors in sequence has yet another flaw. If one avoids making Nero the sixth by beginning with Augustus, Galba becomes the "one [who] is." Galba's reign (68–69), however, ran its course before the temple in Jerusalem was destroyed. It is quite unlikely, therefore, that Revelation was written under Galba. Some interpreters who begin the series with Augustus do not accept the logical conclusion that Galba is the sixth. They omit Galba, Otho, and Vitellius on the grounds that Suetonius describes their reigns as "a revolution of three emperors" (*rebellio trium principum; Vesp.* 1). But Suetonius' point is not that their reigns were in any way illegitimate, only that they were unstable and that the Flavians brought stability once again. If, therefore, one holds the position that the seven heads represent all the (legitimate) emperors in sequence, one may not leave Galba, Otho, or Vitellius out. All three were successively recognized as emperor by the senate. Suetonius includes them in *The Twelve Caesars,* and they also appear in *Sib. Or.* 5:12–51 and 4 Ezra 11–12.

The first basic position, then, that the seven heads include all the Roman emperors up to the time of the author of Revelation, involves insurmountable difficulties. The second basic position is that the author was not actually writing under the "one [who] is." Most holders of this position assume that the seven heads represent all the emperors in sequence. One form of this theory is that the writer of Revelation made use of a source that had been written under the sixth emperor. Wilhelm Bousset and R. H. Charles attempted to reconstruct this source, but with little success.[27] It is, nevertheless, probable that John used earlier traditions in this chapter and that the reference to seven kings was a traditional element. The motif of a seven-headed beast is certainly traditional.[28] The schema of seven kings may reflect one of the typical Jewish patterns used in ordering large blocks of time. The use of the number seven characterizes one of these patterns. Seven of course was a crucial number for Jews because of the observance of the Sabbath. There may have been a kind of sabbatical logic at work in Jeremiah's prediction that the exile would last seventy (7 × 10) years (Jer. 25:11–12; 29:10). These passages in Jeremiah influenced several later texts. In Daniel 9 the prophecy is reinterpreted as seventy weeks of years (70 × 7). The end of this period was expected to coincide with the new age. Similar logic and calculations can be detected in the

Damascus Document and the Melchizedek scroll from Qumran and in the Testament of Levi 15–16. Periods of time are organized into cycles of seven in the book of Jubilees, in portions of the Enoch literature, and in the Testament of Abraham.[29]

The identification of the seven heads of the beast with seven kings may well be an example of this traditional sabbatical eschatology. A saying to that effect or an earlier form of the vision of Revelation 17 may well have originated in Nero's reign. This date is arrived at by beginning with Julius Caesar and counting consecutively, until the "one [who] is," namely, the sixth. The saying or vision may have been formulated by anti-Roman Palestinian Jews, perhaps among producers of sibylline oracles.

It is unlikely, however, that John simply took over this tradition without applying it to his own situation, as both Bousset and Charles suggest. The remark that the beast who will return is the eighth and belongs to the seven implies that John has made some calculations and that the numbers are meaningful for him.

Thus, the theory that John took over a source or traditional element and reinterpreted it is more plausible than the hypothesis that he incorporated it unthinkingly. We shall return to the question of how he reinterpreted the material that he incorporated.

The theory that the author was not actually writing under the "one [who] is" takes another form, namely, that he antedated his work. The main argument supporting this form of the theory (apart from the desire to harmonize ch. 17 with Irenaeus' dating) is that such antedating is a common device in apocalyptic literature. Many Jewish apocalypses are indeed antedated. But usually the entire work is clearly set in an earlier time and the seer is a venerable figure of the distant past. Revelation does not have these characteristics. The function of antedating is usually to allow for prophecies after the fact, so that the book gains authority. It is unlikely that Rev. 17:10 has such a function. No other passage in the book clearly functions in that way. This passage is too minor and too obscure to be an impressive example of predictive reliability.

The third basic position is that the seven heads do not represent all the emperors who reigned up to the author's time, but only a selection. E.-B. Allo argued that the heads represent consecutive emperors beginning with Nero, the first to show open hostility to the church.[30] A. Strobel theorized that the first head is Caligula. He argued that Rev. 17:9–12 reflects a theology of history in which the death and exaltation of Christ constitute the turning point from the old to the new aeon. The list of emperors could only begin, therefore, with the first to come to power after Jesus' death, Caligula (37–41 C.E.).[31] Lyder Brun also concluded that the first head is Caligula. In support of this contention, he pointed to the fact that Caligula was the first emperor to instigate serious trouble for the Jews.[32] The attempt to set his statue up in the temple must have reminded the Jews of the sacrilege of Antiochus Epiphanes. Both Josephus and Philo witness to the deep impression Caligula's policy made.

The fourth basic position is that the seven kings are not intended to be identified with specific historical kings, but are purely symbolic. This theory is unlikely. Given the allusions to the person of Nero, it is doubtful that the identity of the other kings could be passed over without further ado. The number seven was clearly symbolic, as we saw above. But its symbolic character is not incompatible with historical allusion.

It is likely that a theory like those grouped above as the third basic position explains how John reinterpreted his source. Caligula would have been a natural starting point, given the close affinities between Revelation and contemporary Jewish anti-Roman literature and the probable Jewish origin of John. It is impossible to say with certainty what John had in mind. The most likely hypothesis is that he began counting with Caligula and included the following emperors in sequence, omitting Galba, Otho, and Vitellius as reigning too short a time to cause trouble for the saints. The analogy of the eagle vision in 4 Ezra makes it plausible that a selection could have been made of emperors who were especially feared and hated. The five would then be Caligula, Claudius, Nero, Vespasian, and Titus. Domitian would be the "one [who] is." A seventh was expected, to fill out the traditional number seven. The prediction that the last emperor would have a short reign probably arose from the intense expectation of the end of the age in the near future. This logic is rather too cumbersome to explain the passage as John's original composition. It does, however, explain how he would have reinterpreted a source.

The motif of the seven kings does not by any means point decisively to a date earlier than the reign of Domitian for the Apocalypse as a whole. The motif is probably traditional, but the context shows that it was meaningful for the author. This passage does not establish a Domitianic date, but is compatible with such a date.

THE TEMPLE IN JERUSALEM

Revelation 11 opens with the following words: "And a reed like a rod was given to me, saying, 'Get up and measure the temple of God and the altar and the ones who worship in it. But leave out [or cast out] the courtyard which is outside the temple and do not measure it, because it was given to the nations, and they will trample the holy city for forty-two months" (vs. 1–2). Many historical critics have noted that this passage seems to imply that the earthly, historical temple in Jerusalem is still standing. Before the technique of source criticism was applied regularly to Revelation, that is, before 1882, this passage was used to date the book as a whole before 70 c.e.[33]

After the remarks quoted above, the passage in its present form continues: "And I shall give [power or authority] to my two witnesses, and they will prophesy for one thousand two hundred and sixty days, clothed in sackcloth. These are the two olive trees and the two lampstands . . ." (vs. 3–4a). The period of time mentioned here is equivalent to the forty-two months of v. 2. These verses introduce the story of the two witnesses (11:3–13).

Recently, J. A. T. Robinson has revived the argument that Revelation as a whole was written before 70.[34] He sees 11:1–13 as a unity, composed by the author of Revelation. He interprets the measuring as a command that the temple be purified. That purification is part of the final call to repentance issued by the two witnesses. Robinson finds it incredible that the passage was written after the destruction of Jerusalem in 70, since only a tenth of the city falls after the ascension of the witnesses (v. 13) and by an earthquake, not an enemy's attacks.

The first question is whether vs. 1–2 and 3–13 are a unity; that is, whether they were originally composed as a continuous passage. The alternative is that the passage was composed by joining two sources or two separate traditions. The latter alternative is the more probable. The connection between the two is loose and external. The only obvious link is that the scene is Jerusalem in both. The time periods mentioned in each section are equivalent, but the repetition is a seam, as it were, joining the two sources. The first section focuses on the temple, but the second does not mention the temple at all.

The next question that must be raised in considering Robinson's theory is whether the two sections were rather freely formulated by the author of Revelation on the basis of tradition, or whether he adapted oral or written sources whose wording was relatively fixed. In both cases, it is likely that the author was using a source. The references in v. 2 to the outer courtyard and to the Gentiles trampling the courtyard and city make it probable that the first section originally referred to the historical temple in Jerusalem. It is conceivable that v. 1 was originally composed with an allegorical or spiritual meaning.

The temple of God, the altar, and the worshipers in it (presumably the temple) could easily have several layers of meaning. It would not be surprising if a figurative meaning were primary. Verse 2, on the other hand, has much too concrete and historical a surface meaning to have been composed with any other sort of primary reference.

If it is the historical temple which is being discussed, one must then determine what is being said about it. A. Feuillet has argued that the wording of v. 2 makes a historical or literal meaning impossible.[35] How, he asks, could a courtyard be "cast out"? In any case, it is already said to be "outside." The Greek words in question, however, need not be translated in the physical sense. The verb can also have the sense "reject."[36] In this context, "leave out," or "leave aside," would seem to be legitimate translations.

The symbolic act of measuring was used in the Jewish Bible to express a wide variety of meanings: rebuilding, restoring, judgment, destruction, and preservation.[37] Since the image was used for opposite meanings in different contexts, the meaning here must be determined primarily from the context. The outer courtyard is not measured and it is given over to the Gentiles; they will trample the holy city for forty-two months. So the courtyard is at least to be controlled by the Gentiles. Perhaps it is to be profaned or even destroyed as well. Since the outer courtyard is not measured and the temple, altar, and worshipers are measured, the destiny of the latter must be the opposite. So the temple, altar, and worshipers are to escape the control of the Gentiles (and possibly profanation and destruction as well).

The language implies a situation of military conflict.[38] It fits well the situation described by Josephus in the sixth book of *The Jewish War*, when Titus and his legions had broken through the walls of the outer temple by firing the gates. After establishing access to the outer temple, Titus ordered the fire put out and held a council of war with his generals to decide whether or not to destroy the sanctuary itself. The insurgents had made the temple their citadel and had been resisting the Romans from there. Titus decided not to destroy the temple, but his soldiers were carried away by passion and set fire to it against his orders. When the sanctuary was in flames, the soldiers decided they might as well set fire to what remained of the outbuildings. Josephus records the following incident which occurred in the process:

> Next they came to the last surviving colonnade of the Outer Temple. On this women and children and a mixed crowd of citizens had found a refuge —6,000 in all. Before Caesar could reach a decision about them or instruct

his officers, the soldiers, carried away by their fury, fired the colonnade
from below; as a result some flung themselves out of the flames to their
death, others perished in the blaze: of that vast number there escaped not
one. Their destruction was due to a false prophet who that very day had
declared to the people in the City that God commanded them to go up
into the temple to receive the signs of their deliverance. A number of
hireling prophets had been put up in recent days by the party chiefs to
deceive the people by exhorting them to await help from God, and so
reduce the number of deserters and buoy up with hope those who were
above fear and anxiety.[39]

Josephus' negative interpretation of the motives of the prophets he
mentions may be due, at least in part, to his negative judgment on the
Jewish resistance. It is likely that some of those prophets spoke and
acted in good faith. This general context provides a plausible background for the prophecy of Rev. 11:1–2. When the prophecy was not
fulfilled on the literal level, it seems to have been handed on with one
or more new interpretations.

It is unlikely that the author of Revelation in its present form could
have composed 11:1–2. There is no positive interest in the historical,
earthly temple elsewhere in the book. In 3:12 the phrase "the temple
of God" is used in quite a different way. Christ promises that he will
make the one who conquers a pillar in the temple of God. This
language implies that the author of Revelation conceives of the Christian community, either in his own time or in the new age, as the real
or new temple of God. Such a conception is most understandable after
the historical temple had been destroyed. In the visions of the body
of the book, apart from 11:1–2, the temple of God refers to the temple
in heaven (7:15; 11:19; 14:15, 17; 15:5, 6, 8; 16:1, 17). In the final
vision, the vision of the new Jerusalem, it is explicitly stated that there
is no temple in the city (21:22). The lack of a temple probably reflects
the destruction of the historical temple, as well as the attitude that no
restoration of the temple is necessary.

It is also unlikely that the author of Revelation, composing freely,
would have referred to the earthly, historical Jerusalem as "the holy
city" (11:2). The writer's positive concern is for "the new Jerusalem,
which comes down out of heaven" (3:12). It is the heavenly Jerusalem
which the author calls the holy city (21:2, 10). The earthly Jerusalem
is referred to later in ch. 11 as Sodom and Egypt, the place where the
Lord was crucified (v. 8).

The evidence, therefore, is strongly against the theory that Rev.
11:1–2 was composed by the author of the book as a whole, by John
the prophet. There are also good reasons for holding that a source was

used in 11:3–13. The passage contains a significant number of linguistically distinctive elements, compared with the rest of the book.[40] The content of the passage is best understood as John's adaptation of traditional material about the expected conflict in the last days between two prophets of the end time and the final adversary of God and God's people.[41]

The task of dating the source used in 11:3–13 is made difficult by the fact that it was edited by the author of Revelation.[42] Little certainty can be achieved about precisely what should be attributed to the source and what to the author. Reasonable certainty about the use of a source does not imply the ability to reconstruct the source. Robinson argues that the passage presupposes a pre-70 situation; Jerusalem is assumed to be standing.[43] Bousset and Charles were of the same opinion.[44] This assumption is questionable. Much of Jerusalem was indeed leveled by Titus and his troops in 70. But a legion was stationed there, probably with an ancillary civilian population.[45] It is likely that a considerable number of Jews and Christians returned to the city after the war, and that some rebuilding took place.[46] In fact, a setting in Jerusalem after 70 makes sense of the description of the witnesses' foes as (some) from the peoples and tribes and tongues and nations (v. 9) and as those who dwell upon the earth (v. 10). Such descriptions fit Jerusalem better after 70 than before. There is no compelling reason to date either the source or Rev. 11:3–13 in its present form to a time prior to 70 C.E.

Even if the author of Revelation was using sources in 11:1–13, he must have interpreted them in a way that made sense for his own situation. It is likely that the opposition between the church as the true Jews and those Jews who did not accept Jesus as the Christ played some role in the author's understanding of the prophecy of 11:1–2. The references to Jews as a synagogue of Satan in 2:9 and 3:9 attest to the vehemence of his feelings on this subject. But Feuillet seems to go too far in identifying the worshipers in the temple with the church and the outer courtyard with the unbelieving Jews.[47] There is little support for such an explicit allegorical interpretation elsewhere in the book. It seems more likely that the author reinterpreted the inner/outer distinction of the text with his own heavenly/earthly polarity. The outer courtyard would then represent the earthly Jerusalem and temple which have been given over to the Gentiles. The temple itself, with the altar and the worshipers, would represent the heavenly temple which the Gentiles cannot control, profane, or destroy. In the background loom the tragic events of 70 C.E. But the symbolic measuring is still a source of hope; not any longer for rescue from the military power of the Romans, but for heavenly vindication. This passage about the fate of the earthly Jerusalem introduces the appearance of the two witnesses. The narrative of vs. 3–13 also reflects tragic events, the death of Jesus and the rejection of his message. But hope is expressed here also. As Jesus was raised, so also will the two witnesses be raised. But this time the resurrection will take place in view of the enemies and they will repent (vs. 11–13). The narrative about the two witnesses probably functioned as a paradigm of their own destiny for the earliest readers of Revelation. We will consider the function of this and other narratives in Chapter 5, "The Power of Apocalyptic Rhetoric."

DOMITIAN AND THE CHRISTIANS

The date a commentator is inclined to assign to Revelation has a good deal to do with his or her understanding of the function of the book. J. A. T. Robinson, for example, dates the book to 68 or 69 C.E. One of his reasons is that the author must have experienced the Neronian persecution firsthand, in Rome itself. He writes, "One thing of which we may be certain is that the Apocalypse, unless the product of a perfervid and psychotic imagination, was written out of an intense experience of the Christian suffering at the hands of the imperial authorities, represented by the 'beast' of Babylon."[48] Robinson makes a large assumption and seems to forget how relative "an intense experience" can be. Other interpreters date the book of Revelation to the time of Domitian and argue that there was or must have been massive and systematic persecution of Christians during his reign.[49]

The evidence for persecution of Christians under Domitian is rather slight. Doubt is cast on the early Christian tradition about Domitian as the second persecutor by its probable apologetic function.[50] The persons named as victims of this persecution seem to have been, at most, sympathizers of Judaism or God-fearers. The conclusion that they were Christians is unwarranted.[51] Suetonius praises Nero for his repression of the Christians. If Domitian also had taken steps against Christians as such, Suetonius would probably have mentioned the fact.[52]

A number of other early Christian texts are referred to often as further evidence for a persecution under Domitian. First Peter clearly reflects some degree of persecution, but its date is uncertain.[53] The allusion to Rome as Babylon shows that it was written after 70 C.E. But there is no compelling reason to prefer a Domitianic date to other possibilities. Nothing in Hebrews points to more than the usual harassment to which Christians were exposed from time to time in the first two centuries. The allusion to misfortunes and calamities *(symphoras kai periptōseis)* in *1 Clement* 1 is so vague that it need not refer to persecution at all.

There seems, therefore, to be no reliable evidence supporting the theory that Domitian persecuted Christians as Christians. Nevertheless, as indicated in connection with the letter to the Hebrews above, Christians were harassed from time to time in the first two centuries. The fact that the founder of the Way had been crucified by the Romans already in itself made the earliest Christians and their communities suspect. The letters of Paul and the book of Acts attest to a pattern of events that begins with controversy between Christians and Jews and leads, via Jewish initiative, to the involvement of Roman officials. Acts 16:16–24 and 19:23–41 suggest that Gentiles sometimes took the initiative in either unofficial harassment or denunciation of Christians to Roman authorities.[54]

The study of the relationship between the early Christians and Roman officials in the first century is very complex and controversial because of the scarcity of evidence.[55] What evidence there is supports the theory of G. E. M. de Ste. Croix that the sporadic actions of the Roman "government" against Christians during this period were due primarily to the pressure of public opinion.[56] This negative public opinion was owing, ostensibly, to the belief that Christians were guilty of certain abominations *(flagitia)* such as incest and cannibalism. De Ste. Croix argues plausibly that such accusations only masked a deeper, truer reason, namely, that the Christians' refusal to worship any god but their own aroused pagan hostility. The pagans feared that this exclusiveness alienated the goodwill of the gods and endangered the well-being of nature and society. Such an attitude is easily demonstrated for the later period and it fits the discussions of Christians by Tacitus, Suetonius, Pliny, and Trajan.

Only a few passages in Revelation clearly look back on persecution in the past. One of these is 1:9, which implies that the author was banished to Patmos because of his activities as a Christian prophet. Another is 2:13, which refers to Antipas' death at Pergamum, probably an execution ordered by the governor of the province of Asia. The vision of the souls under the altar in 6:9–11 may refer to Christians who died before the moment of writing, but such a reference is not certain. The other allusions to persecution in the book cannot be used as evidence for events that have actually occurred or are occurring. The form of the vision account and the use of tenses in the book foreclose any easy conclusions about the relation of these texts to historical reality. It seems safest to conclude that most of the rest of the book expresses the author's expectation of persecution.

The passages that do refer clearly to cases of persecution in the past involve only two people. Further, these events could have taken place at almost any time in the first two centuries after the death of Jesus. There is, therefore, no compelling reason to understand Revelation as a reaction to any new or significant initiative of Roman authorities against Christians.

The theme of persecution in Revelation allows a date during the reign of Domitian but does not establish it in and of itself. Another element in the book that has often been used to date it to Domitian's reign is the motif of ruler cult. It is well known that Augustus followed a moderate policy on this score.[57] He allowed himself to be worshiped (while still living) in the provinces, as long as the cult included the worship of Rome as well. He did nothing to check private expressions of veneration. In Italy divinity could be ascribed to him only after death. Tiberius followed Augustus' precedent. Caligula, on the other hand, presented himself as a god even in Rome and had temples and sacrifices dedicated to his own divinity. He demanded oaths by his own genius and insisted that he be honored by the ritual of *proskynēsis*. The latter was a gesture of greeting offered by a social inferior to his superior. It originated in Persia and was considered as self-abasement by free Greeks and Romans. The act would probably have had connotations of worship as a gesture to a supposed god. Because of the allusions to Nero, Revelation cannot be dated to the time of Caligula. But the prominence of ruler cult in ch. 13, together with the fact that Caligula was the first to exploit it, increases the likelihood that he is the first king of 17:10, in John's view.

Claudius attempted to return to the policy of Augustus, but apparently Caligula had set a new precedent, irresistible for some. Perhaps as flattery, certain Roman writers gave Claudius divine epithets. Nero associated himself closely with Hercules and Apollo and encouraged flattery of himself as divine. A date under Nero for Revelation is excluded by its reflection of his death and the legend of his return. Vespasian and Titus returned to Augustus' example.

The view of Domitian held by many classical and most biblical scholars today is heavily influenced by the negative portrayal of him by Pliny the Younger, Tacitus, Dio Chrysostom, Suetonius, and Juvenal. These authors wrote after Domitian's death during the reigns of Trajan and Hadrian. One of the undesirable qualities they attribute to Domitian is his demand to be addressed as "lord and god" *(dominus et deus)*. A number of classical scholars have argued, however,

that this negative portrayal does not reflect Domitian and his reign
as they actually were. Rather, it is a product of the desire of the
writers named above to please Trajan and to praise his reign as a new
era. The better to flatter Trajan, the more they had to denigrate
Domitian. It now seems probable that Domitian did not demand that
his subjects refer to him as "our lord and god." Writers associated
with Domitian's court do not use the phrase. Rather, it seems to have
been used by those, such as Martial, who were not in the inner circle
and wished to gain access to it. It was used, apparently, in blatant
attempts to flatter and thus gain influence.[58]

It may well have been a widely used technique of flattery in Domitian's reign. Procurators may have used the phrase to show their
loyalty and gain Domitian's favor.[59] If so, it is likely that John was
aware of its use in Asia by Roman officials and local people who
wished to be regarded as friends of Rome. Naturally, he would have
taken great offense at this use for a human being of a phrase that was
a very common designation for God in the Greek Bible. John himself
used it frequently in the book of Revelation (1:8; 4:8, 11; 11:17; 15:3;
16:7; 18:8; 19:6; 21:22; 22:5).

The practice of *proskynēsis,* introduced by Caligula, was revived by
at least one person who wished to flatter Domitian. According to Dio
Cassius, a certain Juventius Celsus was suspected of conspiracy by
Domitian and saved himself by performing *proskynēsis* and calling the
emperor "lord and god."[60] The gesture allowed by Caligula and
Domitian may be alluded to in Revelation's statements that people
worship *(proskyneō)* the beast (13:4, 8, 12; 14:9, 11; 20:4).

From the time of Augustus it had been the custom to take an oath
by the genius of the emperor. This act was voluntary and not official.
There is evidence that under Domitian for the first time people began
to swear by the genius of the living emperor in public documents.
Flatterers apparently began to offer sacrifice voluntarily to Domitian's
genius.[61]

During Trajan's reign some Christians were denounced before
Pliny the Younger, who was then the governor of Bithynia and Pontus. This incident occurred in about 112 C.E. Some of them denied that
they were Christians. Using what was apparently a standard test,
Pliny asked them to repeat after him an invocation of the gods, to offer
wine and incense to images of Trajan and of the gods, and to curse
Christ (*Epist. ad Traj.* 10.96). M. P. Charlesworth hypothesized that
Domitian made the voluntary action of sacrificing to the genius of the
living emperor into a test of loyalty. Anyone accused or suspected of
disloyalty could save himself or herself by offering sacrifice before the

image of the emperor. If a person refused, he or she could be charged with *atheotēs* (neglect of the worship of the gods).[62] If, however, de Ste. Croix is correct in asserting that the reason Christians were persecuted was their neglect of the worship of the gods, the test described by Pliny could have originated quite spontaneously in the provinces. Then the worship of the emperor, from the pagan point of view, would have been quite an incidental matter. The already long tradition of imperial cult, especially in the form initiated by Caligula, would have encouraged the inclusion of the living emperor's image among those of the other gods, but the worship of the emperor would not have been the central point.

The persecution reflected in Revelation, the banishment of the author and the execution of Antipas, seems to be nothing more than an example of the usual sporadic repression suffered by the Christians in the first two centuries. It is doubtful that the emperor cult was forced upon Christians at any time during the first and early second centuries, including the reigns of Domitian and Trajan. The book of Revelation cannot be understood as a response to a new initiative against the Christians taken by Roman authorities. A more plausible view of its function is that it was written to awaken and intensify Christian exclusiveness, particularly vis-à-vis the imperial cult. The remark in Rev. 13:15, that the beast from the land caused to be slain those who would not worship the image of the beast from the sea, is probably a purposely selective view of the standard cultic test described by Pliny. It is well known that the cities of Asia Minor supported the imperial cult enthusiastically.[63] After persistently seeking the honor, Ephesus was allowed to establish a temple and cult of Domitian as a god *(theos)* during his lifetime.[64] The tendency to flatter Domitian by giving him divine honors and worshiping his person was probably the occasion for the author of Revelation to view the Roman emperor as the adversary of God on the model of Antiochus Epiphanes (Daniel 7-12).

THE SEVEN MESSAGES

Before considering the evidence of the seven messages for the date of Revelation, one must discuss the question of their literary relationship to the rest of the book. R. H. Charles concluded that they were written by the same author as the body of the work, because of the similarity in diction and idiom. He also concluded that they were written earlier than the other portions of Revelation.[65] His major warrant for this conclusion was that the messages contain two conflicting expectations of the end of the world. On one hand, the congregations are expected to survive until Christ's last advent. This idea, according to Charles, is expressed in the exhortation to some in Thyatira "to hold fast what you have until I come" (2:25) and in the warning "I will come as a thief" (3:3). On the other hand, the promise to the congregation in Philadelphia, "I will keep you from the hour of trial which is about to come upon the whole earth to test those who dwell upon the earth," presupposes, according to Charles, a worldwide persecution in which all the faithful would suffer martyrdom. Charles interpreted 3:10 in the light of ch. 7 and other passages. He argued that the 144,000 are sealed to preserve them from demons, but not from physical death. Charles felt that the expectation of survival until the parousia and the expectation of universal martyrdom were mutually exclusive. Therefore, 3:10 must be a later addition to the messages, from a time when the author's expectations had changed.

Charles was probably correct in concluding that certain statements in the seven messages reflect the expectation that some Christians would survive until the parousia. But his thesis that chs. 4–22 presuppose the martyrdom of all Christians goes beyond the evidence.[66] If the author did not expect all Christians to die in a worldwide persecution, the contradiction evaporates.

Charles also put forward a supporting argument for the theory that the messages are earlier than the rest of the book. He interpreted Revelation to mean that a worldwide persecution was to arise in connection with the imperial cult. He found no reference to that cult in the messages, a fact that led him to conclude that they must have been written "before the fundamental antagonism of the Church and the State came to be realized."[67]

In the discussion of the imperial cult above, it was argued that the persecutions already experienced by Christians were not due primarily to conflict between Christians and Roman authorities over the imperial cult. The punitive actions of the Roman officials had the usual, more general causes. The emphasis on the imperial cult in Revelation is probably due to the author's selection of that issue as a negative rallying point for Christians. If the imperial cult was not an objectively significant problem for the congregations in Asia Minor, it is not surprising that it receives little emphasis in the messages. It was suggested above that the author's intention in polemicizing against the ruler cult was to heighten the exclusiveness of Christians vis-à-vis pagan culture. If that suggestion is correct, then the functions of the body of the book and the messages are similar. A major concern of the messages is to refute the position of the Nicolaitans, "Balaam," and "Jezebel." These people apparently were teaching the Christians in Ephesus, Pergamum, and Thyatira to accommodate themselves to the pagan culture for economic, political, and social reasons. This interpretation of the teaching of John's rivals will be presented in Chapter 3.

Charles's theory that the messages were composed earlier than the rest of the book led him to incline toward the theory that they were originally seven letters actually sent to the seven congregations.[68] To make this theory plausible, he had to hypothesize that the endings and parts of the beginnings of the messages were added later to link them with the rest of the book.[69] There is little evidence to support such a theory and its correlative hypothesis. The messages lack the conventional opening and closing of contemporary letters. They are highly stylized and all have the same form. It seems more reasonable to suppose that they were composed for their present context.[70]

The seven messages contain little that points to a date with any precision. In his letter to the Philippians, Polycarp states, "For concerning you he [Paul] boasts in all the churches who then alone had known the Lord, for we had not yet known him" (11:3). Polycarp, bishop of Smyrna in the first half of the second century, implies that the congregation in Smyrna was founded later than the one in Philippi. Some commentators argue on this basis that the message to Smyrna, and thus Revelation as a whole, could not have been written as early as the 60s.[71] This argument is not compelling, but Polycarp's remark does favor a date after 70 for Revelation.

In the message to Smyrna, the following remark is made in reference to the local Jews: "and [I know] the blasphemy of those who say that they are Jews, and are not, but are a synagogue of Satan" (2:9). A similar comment is made about the Jews of Philadelphia (3:9). These comments imply great hostility between at least some Christians and Jews of Asia Minor. At the same time, the author of Revelation, perhaps along with other Christians also, claimed the name "Jew" for himself and his fellow Christians. Robinson argues that such a claim presupposes a time when "the final separation of Christians and Jews had not yet taken place."[72] He apparently believes that the final separation occurred in 70 C.E. with the destruction of the temple. Günter Stemberger argues that the definitive break, from the Christian point of view, took place with the acceptance of the Gentile mission.[73] Other scholars consider the so-called Synod of Jamnia, dated between 80 and 90, to be the turning point.[74] The separation between Jews and Christians cannot be understood as a simple event that took place at a single moment in time and which held for every locality. The separation was gradual and very likely relative to individual perceptions and to the particular circumstances of each geographical area. The indirect claim in Rev. 2:9 and 3:9 that Christians are the true Jews is not a reliable indication of date.

Laodicea suffered a serious earthquake in 60/61 C.E. Nevertheless, it is addressed in Revelation as an affluent church. The earthquake is not mentioned or alluded to in Revelation. These facts have been used by different scholars to support widely differing dates.[75] The fact that the citizens did not need imperial help to rebuild is an indication that a date in the late 60s is not impossible. This bit of evidence is of no positive help in dating the book.

CONCLUSION

The strongest external evidence for the date of Revelation is the testimony of Irenaeus. He says that the Apocalypse was seen at the end of the reign of Domitian. This comment refers to a date of 95 or 96 C.E. It is not clear whether Irenaeus believed that the text was written down at the same time or somewhat later. Since there is no positive evidence for a later date, it seems best to consider Irenaeus' remark to support a date of about 95 or 96 C.E.

The clearest internal evidence in Revelation is the use of the name Babylon for Rome. In Jewish literature this name is explicitly associated with Rome as the second destroyer of Jerusalem. The symbolic name Babylon for Rome was probably taken over by the author of Revelation from Jewish tradition. Its use thus indicates a date after 70 C.E.

The motif of the seven kings in ch. 17 can be interpreted in a variety of ways. The usual assumption that they represent all the emperors up to the author's time leads to insurmountable difficulties. Further, it is not necessarily supported by the parallel texts usually cited. There are insufficient grounds for holding that the author antedated his work. The most likely solution is that John made use of an earlier source in 17:10 and that he reinterpreted it to make sense in his own time. From his point of view, the seven kings were selected emperors, beginning with Caligula, the first to come into significant conflict with the Jews and the first to present himself as a god in his own lifetime in Rome. The king "[who] is" is probably Domitian.

The prophecy in 11:1–2 that the temple would in some sense be preserved from the Gentiles refers to the historical temple in Jerusalem and constitutes a source taken over by the author of Revelation. It dates just prior to the destruction of the temple. John interpreted it in terms of the heavenly temple. The narrative about the two witnesses (11:3–13) is also based on a source, but that source need not be dated prior to 70.

There is insufficient evidence to warrant the conclusion that Domitian persecuted Christians as Christians. The past incidents of persecution reflected in Revelation are best explained as typical of the sporadic opposition encountered by Christians in the first two centuries. It is doubtful that the emperor cult was forced on Christians at any time in the first or early second centuries, including the reigns of Domitian and Trajan. But the practice of the ruler cult by those who wished to flatter Domitian seems to have been the occasion for John to call for intensified Christian exclusiveness over against the surrounding Greco-Roman culture.

The seven messages were probably composed at about the same time as the rest of the work. Their lack of emphasis on the imperial cult is not surprising, if that cult was not being forced on Christians systematically. The messages nevertheless function in a way similar to the visions. They attack the policy of accommodation apparently supported by the Nicolaitans, "Balaam," and "Jezebel" and thus reinforce Christian exclusiveness.

The use of the name of Babylon for Rome and the use of temple language for phenomena other than the physical temple are internal indications of a date after 70. No compelling reason exists to reject Irenaeus' testimony to the date. Ambiguous passages with relevance for the date can be interpreted plausibly against the background of Domitian's reign. That background provides a credible context for the book's content and function.

Many interpreters of Revelation have seen it as a book of consolation written for Christians suffering persecution by order of Domitian. Some have argued that the persecution included the attempt to force Christians to worship the emperor. Both these conclusions imply that John wrote his book as a response to pressing external circumstances. The discussion in this chapter has shown that both these conclusions are false. The implication is that John took a more active role than usually is thought. Rather than simply consoling his fellow Christians in a situation of grave crisis, he wrote his book to point out a crisis that many of them did not perceive. What constituted a crisis in John's view is the subject of the next chapter.

NOTES

1. Irenaeus, *Adv. Haer.* 5.30.3. For an English translation of the passage and its context, see A. Roberts and F. Donaldson (eds.), *The Ante-Nicene Fathers* (Buffalo: Christian Literature Co., 1886), Vol. 1, pp. 559–560.

2. Henry B. Swete, *The Apocalypse of St. John,* 3d ed. (London: Macmillan & Co., 1909), pp. cc–cci.

3. The ancient texts are quoted by Swete (ibid., lxxxix–xc) and R. H. Charles, *A Critical and Exegetical Commentary on the Revelation of St. John,* ICC (Charles Scribner's Sons, 1920), Vol. 1, pp. xcii–xciii.

4. Charles, *A Critical and Exegetical Commentary on the Revelation of St. John,* Vol. 1, p. xcii.

5. See J. A. T. Robinson, *Redating the New Testament* (Westminster Press, 1976), p. 222.

6. Eusebius, *Hist. Eccl.* 4.26.

7. Juvenal, *Sat.* 4.38; Pliny, *Paneg.* 53.3–4.

8. J. Moreau argued that Eusebius used one or more pagan sources listing Roman aristocrats exiled by Domitian and claimed these as Christian victims of persecution ("A propos de la persécution de Domitien," *La Nouvelle Clio* 5 [1953], p. 125).

9. Margaret S. Drower, "Babylon (1)," *OCD,* p. 129.

10. Ibid., "Babylon (2)."

11. Charles, *A Critical and Exegetical Commentary on the Revelation of St. John,* Vol. 2, p. 69; G. B. Caird, *A Commentary on the Revelation of St. John the Divine* (Harper & Row, 1966), p. 216.

12. C.-H. Hunzinger, "Babylon als Deckname für Rom und die Datierung des I. Petrusbriefes," in H. G. Reventlow (ed.), *Gottes Wort und Gottes Land: Hans-Wilhelm Hertzberg zum 70. Geburtstag* (Göttingen: Vandenhoeck & Ruprecht, 1965), pp. 67–77.

13. 2 Esdr. 3:1–2, 28–31; *2 Apoc. Bar.* 10:1–3; 11:1; 67:7; *Sib. Or.* 5:143, 159.

14. Hermann Gunkel, *Schöpfung und Chaos in Urzeit und Endzeit: Eine religionsgeschichtliche Untersuchung über Gen 1 und Ap Joh 12* (Göttingen: Vandenhoeck & Ruprecht, 1895).

15. Adela Yarbro Collins, *The Combat Myth in the Book of Revelation,* Harvard Dissertations in Religion 9 (Scholars Press, 1976), pp. 170–186.

16. C. C. Torrey, *The Apocalypse of John* (Yale University Press, 1958), p. 66; J. M. Ford, *Revelation,* AB (Doubleday & Co., 1975), p. 290; Robinson, *Redating the New Testament,* pp. 248–253; A. A. Bell, "The Date of John's Apocalypse: The Evidence of Some Roman Historians Reconsidered," *NTS* 25 (1979), pp. 93–102.

17. Charles, *A Critical and Exegetical Commentary on the Revelation of St. John,* Vol. 2, p. 69; Wilhelm Bousset, *Die Offenbarung Johannis,* 5th ed. (Göttingen: Vandenhoeck & Ruprecht, 1896), pp. 478–480.

18. T. F. Glasson, *The Revelation of John* (Cambridge University Press, 1965), p. 99; P. Carrington, *The Meaning of the Revelation* (London: S.P.C.K., 1931), pp. 283–284.

19. A. Feuillet, *L'Apocalypse: Etat de la question* (Paris: Desclée de Brouwer, 1963), pp. 77–79; William Barclay, *The Revelation of John* (Westminster Press, 1960), Vol. 2, p. 190; Swete, *The Apocalypse of St. John,* p. 221.

20. E.-B. Allo, *Saint Jean: L'Apocalypse,* 4th ed. (Paris: J. Gabalda, 1933), p. 281; L. Brun, "Die römischen Kaiser in der Apokalypse," *ZNW* 26 (1927), pp. 128–151; A. Strobel, "Abfassung und Geschichtstheologie der Apokalypse nach Kap. XVII. 9–12," *NTS* 10 (1964), pp. 433–445; B. Reicke, "Die jüdische Apokalyptik und die johanneische Tiervision," *RSR* 60 (1972), pp. 173–192.

21. I. T. Beckwith, *The Apocalypse of John* (Macmillan Co., 1919), p. 708; E. Lohse, *Die Offenbarung des Johannes,* 8th ed. (Göttingen: Vandenhoeck & Ruprecht, 1960), p. 87; Caird, *A Commentary on the Revelation of St. John the Divine,* pp. 218–219; M. Kiddle and M. K. Ross, *The Revelation of St. John* (London: Hodder & Stoughton, 1940), pp. 350–351.

22. J. M. Myers, *I and II Esdras,* AB (Doubleday & Co., 1974), pp. 299–301.

23. Yarbro Collins, *The Combat Myth in the Book of Revelation,* p. 175.

24. The translation is by K. Wellesley (Penguin Books, 1964), p. 21.

25. Translation from LCL.

26. Bell, "The Date of John's Apocalypse," p. 98.

27. Bousset, Die Offenbarung Johannis, pp. 478–480; Charles, A Critical and Exegetical Commentary on the Revelation of St. John, Vol. 2, pp. 59–60.

28. Yarbro Collins, The Combat Myth in the Book of Revelation, pp. 77, 79.

29. Adela Yarbro Collins, "Numerical Symbolism in Jewish and Early Christian Apocalyptic Literature," ANRW II.21.2 (forthcoming).

30. Allo, Saint Jean: L'Apocalypse, p. 281.

31. Strobel, "Abfassung und Geschichtstheologie der Apokalypse nach Kap. XVII. 9–12," pp. 437–439.

32. Brun, "Die römischen Kaiser in der Apokalypse," pp. 136–138.

33. Bousset, Offenbarung Johannis, pp. 128, 147.

34. Robinson, Redating the New Testament, pp. 238–242.

35. A. Feuillet, "Essai d'interprétation du chapître XI de l'Apocalypse," NTS 4 (1957–58), pp. 186–187.

36. LSJ (9th ed., 1940), p. 501.

37. Charles, A Critical and Exegetical Commentary on the Revelation of St. John, Vol. 1, pp. 274–276.

38. This was seen by J. Wellhausen; his work is cited by Charles, ibid., p. 270.

39. Josephus, The Jewish War, 6.283–286. Tr. by G. A. Williamson, rev. ed. (Penguin Books, 1970), p. 348.

40. Charles, A Critical and Exegetical Commentary on the Revelation of St. John, Vol. 1, pp. 271–273; Yarbro Collins, The Combat Myth in the Book of Revelation, p. 195n60.

41. Bousset, Offenbarung Johannis, pp. 382–387.

42. Yarbro Collins, The Combat Myth in the Book of Revelation, p. 196n61.

43. Robinson, Redating the New Testament, pp. 240–242.

44. Bousset, Offenbarung Johannis, p. 386; Charles, A Critical and Exegetical Commentary on the Revelation of St. John, Vol. 1, p. 271.

45. E. M. Smallwood, *The Jews Under Roman Rule* (Leiden: E. J. Brill, 1976), pp. 346, 433.

46. G. Stemberger wants to minimize the evidence, but cites it nevertheless; see "Die sogenannte 'Synode von Jabne' und das frühe Christentum," *Kairos* 19 (1977), p. 17.

47. Feuillet, "Essai d'interprétation du chapître XI de l'Apocalypse," p. 187.

48. Robinson, *Redating the New Testament,* pp. 230–231.

49. W. G. Kümmel, *Introduction to the New Testament,* 14th ed. (Abingdon Press, 1966), pp. 327–329; E. Schüssler Fiorenza, "Apocalyptic and Gnosis in the Book of Revelation and Paul," *JBL* 92 (1973), p. 565n3.

50. Moreau, "A propos de la persécution de Domitien," pp. 121–129; E. M. Smallwood, "Domitian's Attitude Toward the Jews and Judaism," *Classical Philology* 51 (1956), pp. 1–2; G. E. M. de Ste. Croix, "Why Were the Early Christians Persecuted?" *Past and Present* 26 (1963), p. 15.

51. Smallwood, "Domitian's Attitude Toward Jews and Judaism," pp. 1, 7–9; Bell, "The Date of John's Apocalypse," pp. 94–96.

52. So also Bell, "The Date of John's Apocalypse," p. 96.

53. E. G. Selwyn, "The Persecution in 1 Peter," *Bulletin of the Studiorum Novi Testamenti Societas* I (1950; reissued in a single volume with numbers 2–3 [1963]), pp. 39–50.

54. See the discussion of Acts 16:19–40 by A. N. Sherwin-White, *Roman Society and Roman Law in the New Testament* (Oxford: Clarendon Press, 1963), pp. 78–83.

55. See the summary of the history of scholarship and the proposed solution by A. N. Sherwin-White, "The Early Persecutions and Roman Law," Appendix V of *The Letters of Pliny: A Social and Historical Commentary* (Oxford: Clarendon Press, 1966), pp. 772–787.

56. De Ste. Croix, "Why Were the Early Christians Persecuted?" pp. 6–38. See the response by Sherwin-White ("Why Were the Early Christians Persecuted—An Amendment") and the reply by de Ste. Croix ("Why Were the Early Christians Persecuted—A Rejoinder") in *Past and Present* 27 (1964), pp. 23–27 and 28–38.

57. For a summary of ruler cult from Augustus through Domitian, see M. P. Charlesworth, "Some Observations on Ruler-Cult Especially in Rome," *HTR* 28 (1935), pp. 26–42.

58. I am grateful to Prof. Leonard Thompson for allowing me to see his as yet unpublished essay "Domitian in Trajan's Ideology."

59. Suetonius, *Domitian* 13.

60. Kenneth Scott, *The Imperial Cult Under the Flavians* (Stuttgart: W. Kohlhammer, 1936; repr. New York: Arno Press, 1975), p. 111; Charlesworth, "Some Observations on Ruler-Cult," pp. 18–19, 33.

61. M. P. Charlesworth, *CAH* 11.42; also see "Some Observations on Ruler-Cult," p. 33.

62. Charlesworth, *CAH* 11.42; also see "Some Observations on Ruler-Cult," pp. 32–34.

63. Swete, *The Apocalypse of St. John*, pp. lxxxix–xci.

64. Scott, *The Imperial Cult Under the Flavians*, p. 96.

65. Charles, *A Critical and Exegetical Commentary on the Revelation of St. John*, Vol. 1, pp. 37–46.

66. I. H. Marshall, "Martyrdom and Parousia in the Revelation of John," *Studia Evangelica* 4, ed. by F. L. Cross (Berlin: Akademie Verlag, 1968), p. 332.

67. Charles, *A Critical and Exegetical Commentary on the Revelation of St. John*, Vol. 1, p. 44.

68. Ibid., pp. 46–47.

69. Ibid., pp. 44–46.

70. So also F. Hahn, "Die Sendschreiben der Johannesapokalypse," in G. Jeremias et al. (eds.), *Tradition und Glaube. Das frühe Christentum in seiner Umwelt. Festgabe für Karl-Georg Kuhn zum 65. Geburtstag* (Göttingen: Vandenhoeck & Ruprecht, 1971), p. 362.

71. This argument is criticized by Robinson, *Redating the New Testament*, pp. 229–230.

72. Ibid., pp. 227–228.

73. Stemberger, "Die sogenannte 'Synode von Jabne' und das frühe Christentum," p. 19.

74. J. L. Martyn, *History and Theology in the Fourth Gospel* (Harper & Row, 1968), pp. 31–41; R. E. Brown, *The Community of the Beloved Disciple* (Paulist Press, 1979), p. 22.

75. See the discussion by Robinson, *Redating the New Testament,* p. 230.

3

The Social Situation–
Perceived Crisis

Apocalyptic literature is often defined as literature evoked by a crisis. The book of Daniel, the Apocalypse of Ezra (4 Ezra = 2 Esdras 3–14), and the Syriac Apocalypse of Baruch *(2 Baruch),* for example, were written during or shortly after grave crises faced by the Jewish people. The book of Revelation also seems to have been written in response to a major crisis. Interpreters of the book, however, disagree on the nature and extent of the crisis. Revelation has long served as the primary evidence for a persecution of Christians under Domitian, but, as we saw in the last chapter, the existence of such a persecution is very doubtful. The lack of supporting evidence for a Domitianic persecution has led at least one interpreter to revive the theory of an earlier date. Most interpreters seem to assume that the occasion of the book must have been an objectively intense and extensive crisis of which the author had personal experience. This axiom can be questioned from the perspective of recent psychological, sociological, and anthropological studies. *Relative,* not absolute or objective, deprivation is a common precondition of millenarian movements. In other words, the crucial element is not so much whether one is actually oppressed as whether one *feels* oppressed.[1]

ELEMENTS OF CRISIS

If the conclusion of the last chapter is correct, that Revelation was written at the end of Domitian's reign (95–96 C.E.), is it appropriate to speak of a crisis that led John to write, and, if so, what was the character of that crisis? A number of elements in the work clearly imply that the author perceives and is responding to a social crisis with several facets.

CONFLICT WITH JEWS

At first, followers of Jesus and believers in Christ considered themselves to be and were perceived by Gentiles as part of that complex diversity we speak of as ancient Judaism. The controversies between followers of Jesus and other Jews brought more and more to public attention the differences between them. The awareness of difference probably created a crisis of identity for at least some believers in Christ. It also made the public status of Christian groups precarious. There was in the early empire a strong suspicion of new religions. Only those firmly rooted in an ethnic tradition and homeland were acceptable. Christians of course had no ancient tradition, no national identity, and no homeland or religious center besides those of the Jews.

John's attitude toward Jews and Judaism was complex and ambiguous; one might even say it was ambivalent. Revelation contains evidence that controversies between believers in Christ and local Jews had created a social crisis for at least some Christians in Asia, probably especially for those, like John, who were Jews by birth or who had earlier become proselytes. The body of the message to Smyrna reads, "I know your tribulation and your poverty (but you are rich) and the slander of those who say that they are Jews and are not, but are a synagogue of Satan. Do not fear what you are about to suffer. Behold, the devil is about to throw some of you into prison, that you may be tested, and for ten days you will have tribulation. Be faithful unto death, and I will give you the crown of life" (2:9–10). The hostility and tension are high, but the break seems rather recent and not entirely irreparable. The name "Jews" is denied to the Jewish community in Smyrna. There is no good reason to think here of Judaizers rather than actual Jews of the local synagogues. Jewish hostility to the early Christian missionary effort is well attested for both the first and the second century.[2] The name "Jews" is denied them because the followers of Jesus are held to be the true Jews. The name "Jew" has not become a term for the distant other, derogatory in and of itself, as it has in much of the Gospel of John. The juxtaposition of the attack on the Jews with the exhortation about persecution suggests that the Roman authorities were being pressed by certain representatives of the local Jewish community to take action against Christians in Smyrna. If that inference is correct, it is probable that followers of Jesus who were also Jews had already been excluded from the synagogues of Smyrna in one way or another. Christians in Smyrna thus no longer enjoyed the social, economic, and political security afforded by association with and attachment to the local Jewish community. The message to Philadelphia begins: "The words of the holy one, the true one, who has the key of David, who opens and no one shall shut, who shuts and no one opens. I know your works. Behold, I have set before you an open door, which no one is able to shut; I know that you have but little power, and yet you have kept my word and have not denied my name. Behold, I will make those of the synagogue of Satan who say that they are Jews and are not, but lie—behold, I will make them come and bow down before your feet, and learn that I have loved you" (3:7–9). Christ, as the speaker of this message, is described as the one "who has the key of David, who opens and no one shall shut, who shuts and no one opens." This description is probably an allusion to Isa. 22:22, where the possessor of the key of David is the king's steward, who decides who will have access to the king and who will not. Applied to Christ, the imagery suggests that Christ is the only one who can grant access to God; he is the only mediator. The reference to an open door which Christ has placed before the Philadelphians and which no one can shut has been interpreted in various ways. Immediately following is an attack on the Jewish community at Philadelphia, similar to the one in the message to Smyrna. In the light of this juxtaposition, the door placed by Christ should be interpreted analogously to the key of David. Christ has given the Christians at Philadelphia access to God and no one can deprive them of it. They are still in relation to God, even though they have been excluded from the synagogues of their city. This imagery implies that the split between Christians and Jews, the exclusion of Christians from the synagogue and all that went with it, was a relatively recent event. In any case, there was still concern among Christians about its negative effect on them. As in the message to Smyrna, there is an implicit claim to the name "Jews."

A similar ambivalence is evident with regard to Jerusalem. On the one hand, the historical city is rejected by the use of the pejorative symbolic names "Sodom" and "Egypt" in 11:8. The crucifixion of Jesus is mentioned in the immediate context, and it is likely that the author interpreted the destruction of Jerusalem as punishment for the rejection of the Messiah. On the other hand, the two witnesses are expected to appear in Jerusalem. After their ministry, a great earthquake will strike the city (Jerusalem). A tenth of it will be destroyed and seven thousand people will be killed. The rest will be frightened and will glorify God. This response is in striking contrast to the reactions evoked by the plagues of the trumpets and bowls (9:20–21; 16:11, 21). The positive response associated with Jerusalem may reflect the author's concern for the eventual conversion of the Jews. At least it places Jerusalem in a more positive light than the rest of the world. More significantly, Jerusalem appears as a major symbol of salvation in the book of Revelation (3:12; 21:2, 10).

MUTUAL ANTIPATHY TOWARD NEIGHBORING GENTILES

Rejection by the Jews was especially threatening for Christians because they had little identity apart from Judaism and because their Gentile neighbors despised them too. There is clear evidence for the second century that many Romans and provincials hated Christians for a variety of reasons.[3] The most fundamental was the charge of "hatred of the human race," an accusation which was also made against the Jews. This charge grew out of Christian exclusiveness, the refusal to respect any god but their own, and thus the avoidance of Gentile political and social life. They were also accused of vices and crimes, such as arson, incest, and cannibalism. These charges were made also against other suspect associations, such as the worshipers of Dionysus. According to Tacitus, Nero chose the Christians at Rome as scapegoats for the public anger about the fire, because there was already a widespread animosity against them. These concerns and attitudes of the second century were probably already fairly widespread in the first. A typical example of Gentile hostility for these reasons is reported in Acts 19. The silversmiths fear for their livelihood and easily arouse a mob against the Christians because of the slight they give to Artemis, the goddess of the Ephesians.

Rejected by Jew and Gentile alike, the Christian of Asia Minor was neither fish nor fowl. The literature of Christians from this region in the first two centuries shows a variety of responses to this situation. Within Revelation two responses can be seen at war with one another, John's response and that advocated by the Nicolaitans, "Balaam," and "Jezebel."

The Nicolaitans, as we have seen, were apparently active in Ephesus (2:6) and Pergamum (2:15). Followers of "Balaam" and "Jezebel" are mentioned in the messages to Pergamum and Thyatira. All three groups are presented as holding the same basic teaching and practice. John's criticism of them focuses on their eating meat sacrificed to idols and playing the harlot *(porneusai)*. It is probable, at least for the issue of eating a certain kind of meat, that the literal meaning of the words is intended. It is just as likely, however, that the dispute is not a narrow one over practical problems.[4] Rather, two different perspectives on the relation between faith and culture are at odds. *Porneusai* had come in Jewish tradition to represent idolatry. John uses the word in a metaphorical sense elsewhere in relation to "Babylon."[5] At stake here was the question of assimilation: What pagan customs could Christians adopt for the sake of economic survival, commercial gain, or simple sociability? The social and economic associations of Asia Minor, including the ones organized for basic kinds of assistance of members, had a religious aspect. Such was the case with the trade guilds that were prominent in Thyatira. It has often been suggested that some Christians in that town were probably members of some of those guilds.[6] I. T. Beckwith rejected William Ramsay's suggestion that John was asking such Christians to withdraw from the trade guilds.[7] Beckwith implied that John was simply asking them to avoid compromising their faith while remaining members. But it is not apparent that such a stance was possible, let alone what John had in mind. Unlike Paul, John does not allow for any exceptions to the rule that meat sacrificed to idols must be avoided. Avoiding such meat would have been at best awkward and possibly insulting in pagan social circumstances. Further, it is likely that John understood "harlotry" or idolatry in a broad sense. It is hard to imagine him condoning, for example, membership in the guild of the silversmiths at Ephesus, who honored Artemis, no matter how carefully one avoided actual cultic acts in her honor.

In the face of Greco-Roman suspicion and antipathy toward Christians, the Nicolaitans, "Balaam," and "Jezebel" apparently took the position that Christians should not be so exclusive. That view is rejected by the Christ of the messages. Eating meat sacrificed to idols symbolized for the author of Revelation a stance of openness to the surrounding Greco-Roman culture, an openness that he regarded as syncretistic and therefore idolatrous. The thrust of the Apocalypse is toward even greater exclusiveness, as we shall see in Chapter 4. The threat from without is met by clarifying and intensifying norms within the group. The messages seem well on the way toward the position that deviants from the norms should be expelled.

CONFLICT OVER WEALTH

Social tensions resulting from different degrees of wealth and different attitudes toward wealth are reflected in the book of Revelation. The issue of wealth should not be treated in isolation, but must be seen as one strand in a complex web of social relations and attitudes. Revelation criticizes the Christians of Laodicea for relying on their wealth. It also attacks the Roman Empire for being a source of wealth, most clearly in ch. 18. These attitudes can best be explained within a series of concentric contexts. The widest is the general resistance to Roman rule among subject peoples, especially in the East. Much of this resistance was on economic grounds. The next important context is Jewish polemic against Rome, some of which focuses on the issue of social justice. A further aspect of the historical situation of Revelation significant in this regard was the social unrest in Asia Minor at the time. Much of that unrest grew out of the tension between rich and poor.

a. Resistance to Rome in the East

In ch. 18, Rome is attacked in part simply because some of her citizens and friends are wealthy. Such an attack seems less arbitrary when we remember that John was a resident of the East and apparently was influenced by the many cultural and ethnic tensions and the propaganda of that region. One major cultural tension was Eastern resentment of Roman political rule and the taxes that went with it. Resistance to Rome in the East was largely verbal, what Harald Fuchs has called "geistige Widerstand" (intellectual opposition).[8]

Early in the history of Roman involvement in the East, in 191 B.C.E., a Roman army defeated a descendant of Alexander's successor in Syria, Antiochus III, at Thermopylae in northern Greece. The conflict was over influence in Asia Minor, a struggle eventually won by the Romans. A story circulated in Greek about what happened immediately after the Roman victory at Thermopylae.[9] While the Romans were taking the weapons from the slain among the enemy, a fallen leader of the enemy's cavalry suddenly got up, demanded that the Romans cease defiling the dead, and predicted that Zeus would punish the Romans for their impious deeds. He would send a people against Italy who would wrest power away from the Romans. The story went on to tell of various omens boding ill for Rome. Finally, a Roman consul fell into a trance and predicted that a great army from Asia would lay Italy waste. To show that his prediction was reliable, he prophesied his own end, that he would be torn to pieces by a wolf. His death occurred as predicted. Then his head continued to foretell how men would fall, women and children and all wealth would be taken to Asia as booty. The story ends with the assurance that everything happened just as predicted. Obviously, the story's predictions do not correspond with the events of history. But the existence of the story says a good deal about Eastern hopes for an eventual defeat of Rome and resurgence of Asia. The story was attributed to Antisthenes, a historian from Rhodes in the early second century B.C.E.[10]

Several Greek and Latin authors writing in the first centuries B.C.E. and C.E. mention historians and other writers whom they call enemies of Rome. At least one of these was active at the court of a foreign king. Seneca quotes Timagenes, an Alexandrian, who said that, if Rome went up in flames, he would be sad only because he knew the city would rise up again afterward, even more beautiful than before.[11] Sallust presents Mithridates persuading the Parthian king to join him in resisting the Romans because of their deep greediness for power and wealth.[12] Tacitus placed in the mouth of a British king a complaint probably typical of small peoples dominated by Rome: "Robbing and conquering, finding no more land, they now search for ocean; greedy for goods, when the enemy is rich, greedy for glory, when he is poor, neither in East nor in West to be satisfied. . . . Robbery, murder, and theft are falsely called dominion, and when they create a desert, they call it peace."[13]

b. Jewish Polemic Against Rome

There was diversity in Jewish response to Rome, just as with other peoples. Some early contacts were friendly, and some Jews, especially in the Diaspora, had good reasons for considering the Romans their champions. On the other hand, there had always been an element of opposition to Rome, especially in Palestine. Many Jews apparently identified the fourth kingdom of Daniel with Rome. An anti-Roman saying was attributed to Rabbi Gamaliel, who lived at the turn of the era, "This empire gnaws at our substance through four things: its tolls, its bath buildings, its theaters, and its taxes in kind." As Ramsay MacMullen has said, this saying expresses resentment at both cultural smothering and economic exploitation.[14]

Some of the most virulent verbal attacks on Rome were made by Jews who expressed their feelings in the form of sibylline oracles. Originally a Hellenistic literary form, the sibylline oracle focused on prophecies of future events, often political events. The Romans recognized in the circulation of such oracles a threat to public order and their own power. For example, Augustus had two thousand books of this kind confiscated and burned in 12 B.C.E., according to Suetonius.[15]

The conflict of Asia and Italy was a major theme of the strange story attributed to Antisthenes, which was recounted above. That theme appears also in an oracle preserved in Book 3 of the *Sibylline Oracles:*

> However much wealth Rome received from tribute-bearing Asia, Asia will receive three times that much again from Rome and will repay her deadly arrogance to her.
> Whatever number from Asia served the house of Italians, twenty times that number of Italians will be serfs in Asia, in poverty, and they will be liable to pay ten-thousandfold. (*Sib. Or.* 3:350–355)[16]

The context suggests that Cleopatra was expected to be the champion of Asia after conquering Rome and shifting the center of power from West to East. The date of the oracle is thus before Cleopatra's defeat at Actium in 30 B.C.E., probably not long before.[17] It could have been a pagan composition taken over by a Jew, or a Jewish composition. The main corpus of Book 3 was composed by and for Jews living in Egypt. Thus, whether the oracle was an original Jewish composition or not, it shows that at least one group of Jews in Egypt was aware of propaganda involving a conflict between Asia and Rome and that their sympathies were with Asia.

One of the oracles in the fourth book of the *Sibylline Oracles* reads as follows:

> Great wealth will come to Asia, which Rome itself once plundered and deposited in her house of many possessions.
> She will then pay back twice as much and more to Asia, and then there will be a surfeit of war. (*Sib. Or.* 4:145–148)

This oracle was either composed or taken over by a Jew in about 80 C.E.[18] As noted in Chapter 1, *Sib. Or.* 4 was probably composed in Palestine or Syria. Even apart from the problem of the place of origin, it is unlikely that this oracle expresses the actual conditions in western Asia Minor under the Flavians, as David Magie argued.[19] To be sure, a degree of prosperity did come to parts of the population of the region at that time. Nevertheless, the oracle hardly fits a situation in which Asia Minor was still paying taxes of various kinds to Rome. Indeed, T. R. S. Broughton remarks with regard to Asia Minor, "Vespasian appears to have taken more than he gave."[20] It is more likely that these verses express the typical Eastern resentment of Rome and hope for a reversal of fortunes in the future. It shows once again that Jews shared such feelings with their Eastern neighbors.

Book 5 of the *Sibylline Oracles* is a witness to the political attitudes of at least one group of Jews in Egypt between the Jewish revolts of 70 and 132 C.E.[21] It expresses intense hostility to Rome. The only clear reference to wealth, however, occurs not in the attacks on Rome, but in the description of a heavenly savior:

[he] gave back the wealth to all the good, which previous men had taken. (*Sib. Or.* 5:416–417)

Rome is explicitly criticized, not for greed but for sexual immorality, sorcery, the destruction of Jerusalem, and arrogance (*Sib. Or.* 5: 160–161, 166, 173).

Book 8 of the *Sibylline Oracles* falls into two portions, a collection of political oracles directed mainly against Rome, and a Christologically oriented section. The latter section is clearly Christian. The political portion originally could have been Christian or Jewish, with a slight balance of probability toward the Jewish theory. It was written about 175 C.E. in some part of the Near East subject to Rome.[22] The theme of wealth and poverty is a prominent one in the political portion of this book. It is likely that the theme represents a major social problem in the lives of the author and the intended readers, at least from the author's point of view. Near the beginning we read:

. . . the famous lawless kingdom of the Italians
. . . will show many evils to all men and will expend the toils of the men of all the earth. (*Sib. Or.* 8:9–11)

These lines sound very much like the complaint of a tribute-paying people.

About twenty-five lines later, there is an oracle foretelling the utter destruction of Rome. In between these two denunciations of the imperial city is an admonition against greed. It begins with the remark,

The beginning of evils for all will be love of gain and folly
for there will be a desire for deceitful gold and silver. (*Sib. Or.* 8:17–18)

It ends with the wry comment:

If the huge earth did not have its throne
far from starry heaven, men would not have equal light
but it would be marketed for gold and would belong to the rich,
and God would have prepared another world for beggars. (*Sib. Or.* 8: 33–36)

The placement of this admonition between two oracles against Rome shows clearly that Roman rule was seen to be the root of current economic injustice by whoever gave this section of the book its final form.

In line 50, Rome is addressed as the "luxuriant one," whose kings have enslaved the world from East to West. In line 145, we find the phrase "luxuriant Rome." The Greek words are different, but the ideas involved are very similar to some descriptions of Rome in Revelation 18:

... the wholesale dealers of the earth grew rich from her excessive luxury. (Rev. 9:3)

... as much as she glorified herself and lived luxuriously, to that degree give her torment and mourning. (v. 7)

And the kings of the earth, who prostituted themselves with her and lived in luxury, will weep and mourn over her. (v. 9)

In a long passage in Book 8 of the *Sibylline Oracles,* which depicts future woes on Rome, the following is said:

Woe to you, Italian land, great savage nation.
You did not perceive whence you came, naked and unworthy
to the light of the sun, so that you might go again naked
to the same place and later come to judgment
because you judge unjustly. (*Sib. Or.* 8:95–99)

The implication is that Roman arrogance and greed have led to social injustice.

The emperors Hadrian and Marcus Aurelius are portrayed as greedy and unjust:

Having abundant gold [Hadrian] will also gather more silver from his enemies and strip and undo them. (*Sib. Or.* 8:54–55)

[Marcus Aurelius] will control dominions far and wide, a most piteous king, who will shut up and guard all the wealth of the world in his home, so that when the blazing matricidal exile [Nero] returns from the ends of the earth he will give these things to all and award great wealth to Asia. (*Sib. Or.* 8:68–72)

Here the traditional motif of the reversal of the fortunes of Rome and Asia is combined with the legend of Nero's return.

Books 5 and 8 are strikingly similar in their opposition to Rome. Both make use of the Nero legend. But they are remarkably different in the degree of interest in the problem of wealth and poverty. It seems likely that economic security was not a great problem for the author and intended readers of Book 5. They were either well off or relatively secure and satisfied with their economic lot. The polemics and admonitions of Book 8 do not necessarily imply that the author and intended readers were poor. It is likely that they were relatively disadvantaged. At the very least we can say that something moved the author to comment on the unequal distribution of wealth in his or her society and moved the author to sympathize with those who had less. John the prophet was heir to the tradition of Eastern resistance to Rome in verbal form, both oral and literary. In literary form and in content, John's work is similar to the *Sibylline Oracles,* especially to those portions which are certainly or probably Jewish. John's work is an apocalypse, a form of revelatory literature; the oracle is another form of the same general type. He drew upon certain motifs and themes of the *Sibylline Oracles,* such as opposition to Rome and the legend of Nero's return. Like the Jewish *Sibylline Oracles,* the book of Revelation is a religious work with explicit political attitudes and very definite political implications. The theme of wealth and poverty is not always present in anti-Roman propaganda. It is prominent in Revelation and in Book 8 of the *Sibylline Oracles.* Its prominence in this book is probably due to the relatively disadvantaged status of its author and first readers. Whatever his actual economic situation, the author or editor seems to *feel* that he is a victim of injustice. At the very least, he or she sympathizes with those viewed as unjustly at a disadvantage. It is likely that the theme is prominent in Revelation for the same reasons.

c. Social Unrest in Asia Minor

The book of Revelation was written in Asia Minor at a time of social unrest. One aspect of this unrest was tension between rich and poor. According to the economic historian of the Roman Empire M. Rostovtzeff, there was a continuous struggle in Asia Minor between rich and poor from the time of Vespasian to the rule of Hadrian.[23] C. S. Walton duly noted, as had Rostovtzeff, the brilliant economic progress of Asia Minor in the early empire. But he concluded that the increase in wealth did not affect everyone alike. Those who were well off became millionaires, but the general level of wealth was not raised, with the result that the poor were more discontented rather than less.[24] Ramsay MacMullen and F. E. Peters agree with the assessments of Rostovtzeff and Walton.[25]

MacMullen quotes Plutarch's remark that "the masses are more hostile to a rich man who does not give them a share of his wealth than [to] a poor man who steals from the public funds, for they think that the former's conduct is due to arrogance and contempt of them, but the latter's to necessity."[26] In treating Trajan's reign, David Magie describes a long-standing feud in Smyrna between the men of the upper city and the men of the seashore. He interprets the feud as a conflict between the wealthy and the working classes. He speaks of bread riots in Aspendus, a city of southwestern Asia Minor. The poor rioted because the rich were hoarding grain in hopes of selling it at a large profit. At Tarsus there was a conflict among several groups, two of which were the Council and those who claimed to represent the people.[27] Among the reasons for the unrest was a regulation that anyone whose property fell below a certain level be excluded from the assembly.[28] Another source of tension was the desire of the linenworkers for citizenship. They were freeborn but without the right of franchise.[29]

Perhaps the most vivid and telling example of social unrest at the time of Revelation is an incident in the life of Dio of Prusa, later called Dio Chrysostom, the golden-mouthed. He was born in Prusa in Bithynia, a region of northwestern Asia Minor. His family was wealthy and had high social standing in the city. Originally a Sophist, he was converted to the Stoic and Cynic philosophy. He lived in Rome for some years and was banished by Domitian both from Rome and from his native province in 82. His banishment may have been due to his friendship with Titus Flavius Sabinus, a man whom Domitian eventually killed.[30] He wandered about enduring many hardships, living on alms and his earnings from menial work, until his exile was ended by Nerva. He then returned to his native city and resumed a distinguished career as a politician and orator both at home and abroad.[31]

The incident in question is reflected in Dio's forty-sixth discourse. Magie follows von Arnim in dating the discourse and thus the incident to the period before his banishment, probably in the later years of Vespasian's rule.[32] The price of grain had risen, and, as a consequence, a bread riot had taken place. Magie concludes that the leaders of the city proletariat had incited them against the rich and privileged class.[33] The riot took the form of an attack by the mob on the homes of Dio and a neighbor of his. The intention apparently was to burn the homes and stone the inhabitants to death. The mob turned back suddenly from a narrow lane near Dio's house, presumably because they feared resistance and ambush in that small space. The following morning a town meeting was called by the leaders of the city to discuss the situation. Dio's oration is a protest of the mob's action and a self-defense against their hostility.

From Dio's point of view at least, the people attacked him out of envy and resentment at his having wealth while they were in difficult circumstances. He defended himself in various ways, pointing out, for example, that he was not a producer of grain and denying that he was hoarding any. Some apparently had said that he had money to lend, but was unwilling to supply it for the purchase of grain. He denied that charge as well. He argued that there was resentment against him because he had built colonnades and workshops, apparently for rent, in the city. He asked how such buildings had injured the city and how their construction had increased the price of grain. He openly accused them of envy. Just after that accusation, he became most eloquent.

> Besides, though the matter over which you have become incensed truly does require some attention, still it is not beyond repair or such as to make you act as you are acting. For while the cost of grain has risen higher than what is customary here, it is not so high as to make you desperate. Why, there are cities in which it always is at that price, when conditions are best! There you go, making a tumult once more, as if I were saying it ought to be that price at Prusa too, and never lower. But the point I am making is that, while it is necessary to take steps to make it cheaper, still it is not necessary to feel so bitter over what has happened or to lose your senses; for the way you have acted just now is not the conduct befitting such a matter, nay, if I had murdered your children and your wives you could not have behaved with greater savagery. For to be enraged at one's own fellow citizens—I care not whether justly or unjustly, but at all events at fellow citizens, citizens in good standing, yes, as good as anybody—and not to let them explain or to make an explanation to them, but without more ado to try to stone them and burn their houses, with a view to consuming in one conflagration, if possible, them and their children and their wives—what kind of human beings act that way? In my opinion, I swear by all that's holy, no matter if you will be angry to hear it, such conduct is not that of men in needy circumstances or lacking the necessaries of life. For need develops self-control.[34]

Unfortunately, we do not have a speech from someone on the other side. If, however, Dio was accurate in his remark that the poor were not desperate, we can infer that it was not a matter of survival, not a matter of unquestionable oppression of the poor by the rich, but a difference of opinion on the question of the distribution of wealth, on what was just, fair, and reasonable. The riot seems to have grown out of a sense of being relatively deprived and from a belief that the rich somehow were conspiring against the poor. Dio's remark that need develops self-control sounds very much like an example of the perennial idealizing of poverty by the rich from a safe distance. In Dio's case, however, it is a principle in which he believed deeply. He apparently tested it in his own life later on, during his exile of at least fourteen years.

The riot involving Dio's home was not explicitly anti-Roman, as far as we know. It is perhaps significant, however, that Dio's family had strong Roman connections. His grandfather was a friend of an emperor, perhaps Claudius. Dio says that his grandfather won goodwill toward Prusa from the emperor.[35] Later, Dio himself interceded for the city with Trajan and won certain benefits for its citizens. From Dio's point of view, these Roman connections were helpful to the city. The poor, however, some of whom may not even have been citizens, may have viewed them in a different light.

Dio's values were aristocratic. His hopes for his city centered on its good reputation abroad, its leadership and influence over other cities in the region, and the magnificence of its architecture, especially public buildings, which he hoped would approach the splendor of the great cities of western Asia Minor, such as Ephesus and Smyrna. In his later career, he met much opposition in Prusa to a public building program which he had initiated.[36] Perhaps at least some of the opposition came from those who did not share his cosmopolitan values. Some may have preferred cheaper bread to grand buildings.

Toward the end of the first century and during the first part of the second, there were severe strains between rich and poor in Asia Minor. The book of Revelation was shaped to some extent by those strains, as we will see in the next chapter.

PRECARIOUS RELATIONS WITH ROME

Early Christian communities in the Greco-Roman world had a positive public social identity as unofficial associations like many other *koinōniai* or *collegia* of the day.[37] These societies arose to fill needs unsatisfied by the household and the local government. They apparently always had a religious dimension, the unity of the association finding expression in the worship of a particular deity. Sometimes the members practiced the same craft or trade. They held common funds for charity and provided for the needs of members, such as burial. The early Christians would certainly have been viewed by Roman authorities and Gentiles in general as forming an association of the usual kind. Christians themselves, of course, considered their communities to be a good deal more than this. But in the earlier stages, their organization and customs showed that they based their *public* identity at least on the traditional unofficial association. At first, followers of Jesus and believers in Christ simply belonged either to Jewish associations or to their own, which were understood by Gentiles in terms of the Jewish ones.

This public identity of Christians was threatened in various ways. The authorities often looked with suspicion even on Gentile *collegia*, because they had no official supervision and could become centers of unrest leading to public disorder.[38] In the early second century, Pliny the Younger, while governor of Bithynia and Pontus, wrote to the Emperor Trajan, saying that the city of Nicomedia had no association of fire fighters. Pliny proposed that one be established to protect life and property. Trajan refused to grant his permission, saying that such societies had greatly disturbed the peace and that before long the fire fighters' association would be a political society.[39] In another letter, Pliny referred to the city of Amisus, which was free and confederate, and thus had the privilege of its own laws. Societies for mutual benefit were in existence, and Pliny wrote asking whether these should be allowed to continue. Trajan replied that they could continue, as long as there was no riot or faction, but only the support of the indigent. He added that in cities subject to Roman laws, societies of this sort should be prohibited.[40] Christians in Pontus apparently gave up their communal meals when Pliny issued an edict against associations.[41] The public life of early Christians thus had a recognizable social identity, but to some extent, even because of that identity, their public status was precarious. The fact that their leader, the one from whom they were named, was executed by the Roman prefect of Palestine did not make things any easier for the early Christians.

The first three elements of crisis discussed above, conflict with Jews, mutual antipathy toward neighboring Gentiles, and conflict over wealth, were all local in character. None of them involve direct Roman initiative and intervention. Nevertheless, the Romans were regularly drawn into conflicts of these kinds. If a Jew or a Gentile had a complaint against a Christian, he or she would accuse him or her before the Roman governor. If the poor got unruly, the wealthy citizens could remind them that the Romans considered rioting a crime. It is thus not surprising that some Christians in the region considered the Romans their enemies along with their other opponents who were closer to home.

Revelation does not seem to have been written in response to an obvious, massive social crisis recognized as such by all Christians, not even a regional one. But the social status of Christians in Asia Minor was threatened in several ways. Christians were being ostracized and sometimes accused before the authorities by their Jewish neighbors. Local Gentiles despised and were suspicious of them and were also inclined to accuse them before the magistrates. Some Christian leaders were advocating Christian participation in civic life to counter this antipathy. There was tension between rich and poor which tended to erupt in times of stress and shortage of food. Christians who were poor or disenfranchised, or whose situation was precarious for other reasons, probably sympathized with the poor in these conflicts. Finally, Roman magistrates were often brought in to arbitrate these various social conflicts. They increasingly looked with disfavor upon Christians and condemned their endurance as stubborn disobedience. It is likely that John the prophet was affected deeply by these elements of crisis and that they had an impact on the shape of his book.

EXPERIENCES OF TRAUMA

Another factor in the composition of Revelation is the experience of trauma, both individual and collective, personal and communal. The trauma I speak of is related to the elements of social crisis just described, and like them can be inferred from the pages of Revelation when it is read in the light of its historical situation. Five traumatic events are reflected in the Apocalypse, all of which involve the Romans as adversaries.

As we saw in the last chapter, the "name of mystery," Babylon, refers throughout Revelation to the city of Rome. The name Babylon is used to describe Rome as the second destroyer of the temple and Jerusalem. The frequent and intense use of this symbol suggests that the destruction of Jerusalem was a traumatic event, at least for John himself. The traumatic effects of the event do not seem to have been lessened by the split between Jewish and Christian associations in Asia Minor. One of the conclusions of Chapter 1 was that John was probably a Palestinian. If so, he may have experienced the war with Rome directly. Its effects would have been especially potent on John if he was a resident of Jerusalem when the war broke out. The emotional reaction would have been even stronger if he was a native of Jerusalem. But even if he was not a resident or native of the city, it is likely that its destruction meant the loss of his spiritual and symbolic center. In Revelation, language about a heavenly temple and a new Jerusalem seems to compensate for the loss of the earthly temple and city as a symbolic center. The message to the Philadelphians contains an example: "He who conquers, I will make him a pillar in the temple of my God; never shall he go out of it, and I will write on him the name of my God, and the name of the city of my God, the new Jerusalem which comes down from my God out of heaven, and my own new name" (3:12). The attack on Jerusalem as "Sodom" and "Egypt," and as the place where Jesus was crucified, probably reflects the way in which John, like other believers in Jesus Christ, made sense of the destruction. It was punishment for the rejection of the Messiah.

The negative language is part of the attempt to come to terms with the loss and not a sign of alienation from the city prior to 70. The Emperor Nero is never explicitly named in Revelation. Like the *Sibylline Oracles,* the Apocalypse refers to political figures and events obliquely, symbolically, and mysteriously. A number of images in chs. 11, 13, and 17 are credibly interpreted as alluding to Nero, his propaganda, and legends circulating after his death. This prominence of Nero as an adversary of God and the saints and as a prototype, along with Antiochus Epiphanes, of the Antichrist, reflects the traumatic experience of the arrest, conviction, torture, and execution of Christians in Rome at Nero's behest. These things took place in the mid-60s, following the great fire at Rome. Nero's treatment of the Christians in Rome should probably be seen in the context of the traditional Roman hostility to foreign cults and religious practices thought to have a socially and politically dangerous character.[42] As we have seen, it is likely that his decision was influenced by popular animosity toward Christians.[43] It is improbable that Nero issued a general law prohibiting the Christian faith or that the Senate produced a *senatus consultum* against Christians. It is more likely that Nero acted on the basis of his police power and that the affair was specific and local.[44] Nevertheless it had wider implications and effects. The hatred of the populace of Rome for the Christians was probably typical of the attitudes of the citizens of many provincial cities as well. If the Christians could easily become scapegoats in Rome, the same could happen elsewhere. Secondly, Nero's conclusions about his rights and duties in dealing with Christians in terms of Roman law could have been drawn independently by governors and prefects. Further, Nero's action may have set a precedent.[45] By the time Pliny encountered Christians in Bithynia (about 112), a provincial governor could conclude that it was his duty to execute any unrepentant adult male Christian who was properly accused. Even though Pliny raises the question whether it is the name itself or only the offenses associated with it which are punishable, his decisions on particular cases, which are confirmed by Trajan, show that adherence to the cult is the decisive issue.[46]

It is not surprising that Nero's action against the Christians of Rome was still a traumatic event for Christians living thirty years later in Asia Minor, most of whom were probably not involved directly in the incident. The injustice of the charge and the spectacular brutality of the sentence made the event well known and vivid in memory. The brutality awakened the sympathy even of Romans who despised Christians. The incident would have weighed heavily on the minds of many Christians who had not been there as a striking example of the kind of fate that could befall themselves at any time. Finally, the event was well remembered probably because, as ecclesiastical tradition has it, certain prominent Christian leaders perished in Nero's attempt to protect himself.

Certain analogies support the argument that Nero's action against Christians was still traumatic in John's time. The Apocalypse of Ezra and the Syriac Apocalypse of Baruch are obvious examples of Jewish attempts to deal with the trauma of the destruction of Jerusalem. The current consensus is that they were written about thirty years after the event itself. The continuing attempts by Jews and Christians alike to interpret and respond to the Nazis' atrocities against Jews is a modern example of how traumatic effects are still powerful decades later.

A further trauma was more subtle but nonetheless real. For some Christians of the first and second centuries, just as for some Jews, the imperial ruler cult must have been deeply offensive. The polytheism with which it was joined was equally distasteful. The imperial cult was enthusiastically supported in Asia Minor, often beyond the expectations of the Roman authorities, and sometimes even in conflict with their sensibilities. The public display must have been traumatic for Christians who opposed its ideology deeply and intensely. The trauma was compounded by the fact that their Gentile neighbors resented Christians' rejection of polytheism and ruler cult. The more enthusiastic their neighbors were about ruler cult, the more precarious the Christians' public status became. The effect upon some Christians, on John the prophet, for example, must have been as intense and as negative as the reaction of the Jews of Skokie, Illinois, when the neo-Nazis announced a public march in their town. The Christians of Asia Minor would have been all the more frustrated because their political power was relatively much less, perhaps nonexistent. Another and perhaps closer analogy would be the reaction of black people to a parade or festival openly sponsored by the Ku Klux Klan in a city where black people had no organized political clout.

In the message to Pergamum, the death of Antipas is mentioned. Antipas died "where Satan dwells" (2:13). In the light of chs. 12, 13, and 17, the reference to Satan is a veiled allusion to Roman power. Pergamum was one of the places where the Roman governor held court and made judicial decisions. It may have been the governor's residence in the 90s. The sharp two-edged sword of Christ mentioned in the greeting (2:12) and in the threat (2:16) is contrasted implicitly with the "sword" of the Roman governor, that is, with his power over capital cases.[47] Antipas is called "my witness *(martys),* my faithful

one, who was killed among you." *"Martys"* is not yet a technical term
meaning "martyr" in Revelation. But the description of Antipas associates his death with his witness. Thus it combines the ideas of
verbal testimony and death for the faith. This combination suggests
that Antipas was executed by the Roman governor for being a Christian. He was probably not sought out by the governor, but was accused before him by some hostile Jew or Gentile. This execution was
either recent or notorious among the Christians of Asia Minor, or
perhaps both. It was certainly a traumatic event for Antipas' associates.

In Rev. 1:9 John says that he was on the island of Patmos "on
account of the word of God and the testimony of Jesus." As we saw
in Chapter 1, the most likely interpretation of this remark is that John
suffered some form of Roman repression. Tertullian and Jerome tes-
tify that John's was a case of *relegatio in insulam.*[48] In the imperial
period, *relegatio* was normally banishment for life to a particular
island for specific offenses or because the person involved threatened
the public interest. Among the offenses so punished were the practice
of astrology and the practice of magic *(ars mathematica* and *ars
magica*).[49] Magic was a crime when used with the intent to do harm.[50]
Astrology, divination, and prophecy were often outlawed because
attempts to discern the future were often associated with conspiracy
against the state and often led to disorder.[51] Jewish and Christian
prophecy could be outlawed along with pagan.[52] At some point, for
example, in the first half of the second century, an edict was issued
prohibiting the reading of sibylline oracles and the Jewish prophets.[53]
A provincial governor had the power to pass a sentence of *relegatio.*[54]

Another possibility is that John's sentence was *deportatio in insulam. Deportatio* was more severe than *relegatio* and differed from
it primarily in the forcible removal of the condemned to the place of
exile. *Deportatio* was imposed for a variety of offenses, but was originally applied to political offenders and most often used as a political
measure. The provincial governor could not impose a sentence of
deportatio himself, but could only recommend it in specific cases to
the emperor.[55]

Given Nero's precedent and the death of Antipas, it is somewhat
puzzling that John was banished rather than executed. William Ramsay conjectured that John's sentence could not have been *deportatio,*
but that he was sentenced to hard labor in the quarries of Patmos. His
reasons were that *deportatio* was reserved for persons of standing and
wealth and that it was too lenient a punishment for a Christian at that
time.[56] J. N. Sanders argued that John's was a case of *relegatio,* that

such a sentence was reserved for the aristocracy, Roman or provincial, and that persons were usually relegated to islands far distant from their residences. He concluded that (1) John could not have been expelled from Ephesus; the city in question may have been Jerusalem, Alexandria, or Rome; (2) John must have been a member of the Jewish aristocracy, probably a Sadducee; and (3) he must have been banished before there was precedent for capital punishment of Christians, that is, before 64 C.E.[57]

In support of Ramsay's theory of hard labor is Victorinus' comment that John was condemned to a mine or quarry *(in metallo damnatus)*.[58] But this remark is contradicted by Tertullian and Jerome. The fact that *deportatio* and *relegatio* were normally applied to the upper class is problematic. Sanders' theory that John was a Sadducee is supported by a remark of Polycrates, who was bishop of Ephesus at the end of the second century. He says that John, who reclined on the breast of the Lord and who sleeps at Ephesus, was a priest wearing the plate *(petalon)*.[59] But Polycrates may well have been speaking of another John. Further, the tradition that John was a priest may be a legendary element inspired by John 18:15–16, where "another disciple," possibly the Beloved Disciple, is known to the High Priest. In any case, there may have been exceptions to the practice of banishing only people of high social standing and wealth.

Sanders' argument that John could not have been relegated from Ephesus to Patmos is not compelling. He gives three examples of people being removed to places far distant from the place of expulsion.[60] One of these is Eusebius' reference to Flavia Domitilla's removal from Rome to Pontia, an island opposite Campania. Relative to the other two examples, that removal was of no great distance. It was common practice for the emperors to exile someone from Rome to another mainland city or to an island off the coast of Italy.[61] So, although removal from almost any city of Asia to Patmos would have been a relatively short one, it would by no means have been as unusual as Sanders implies.

The relative leniency of the punishment does not necessarily imply that John was sentenced prior to Nero's execution of Christians in Rome. If there was no general law, the precedent would not have been binding. Individual governors may have varied in their interpretation of the law, of their duties with regard to Christians, and in their susceptibility to public opinion. As we noted earlier, Rev. 2:9 and 3:9 imply that John regarded himself as a true Jew. The Roman official who passed sentence on John may have accepted that self-definition because of his Palestinian origin and knowledge of one or more Semitic languages. Further, if John had come from outside the region, and continued to travel about as an itinerant prophet, and if his prophecy was viewed as a threat to order or Roman authority, the official may have felt that a sentence of banishment was the simplest and most appropriate solution.

John's banishment made evident once again the precarious legal position of Christians, especially those who combined an anti-Roman political perspective with hope for the future and with prophecy. It obviously must have been a traumatic experience for John himself. It is likely that it was at least unsettling for his allies and followers.

CONCLUSION

The traditional view of Revelation is that it was written in response to the second major Roman persecution of Christians, which was initiated by Domitian, a wicked emperor like Nero. As we have seen, Domitian apparently took no steps against Christians as Christians. The examples of Roman repression reflected in Revelation are the sorts of things that could and did happen at various times in the first two centuries C.E. The origin of the Apocalypse, therefore, cannot be explained in terms of a response to that particular kind of social crisis.

A number of recent commentators have argued that it was Domitian's insistence on being worshiped and being addressed as lord and god which provided the stimulus for John's Apocalypse. They would agree that there was no escalation of persecution, but would claim that there were new developments in the imperial ruler cult which moved John to write as he did. One of the conclusions of the last chapter was that Domitian did not demand to be addressed or referred to as lord and god and that he did not make worship of his person a test of loyalty. We did, however, see evidence that the tendency to worship the emperor (formally at least) did increase during Domitian's reign, apparently as an attempt to flatter the emperor and gain security if not influence. The view of Domitian as a new Caligula is just as inaccurate as the portrait of him as a new Nero. Ruler cult had been around for a long time and there was no striking innovation under Domitian. Nevertheless, the fact that a number of people tried to flatter Domitian with divine honors and the fact that he was either unwilling or unable to discourage such a practice were probably significant factors in John's interpretation of his situation. The current practice of ruler cult, as an aspect of John's social situation, is not sufficient in and of itself to explain the origin of the Apocalypse. But if the imperial ruler cult had seriously waned in John's region at his time, his book would look very different, if it would have been written at all.

How do these observations relate to socioscientific theory? In recent studies there has been a convergence of aims and methods on the part of historians, sociologists, and anthropologists in studies of millenarian movements, which are often seen as similar to apocalyptic movements, texts, or mentalities. A number of generalizations have been attempted about the origin of such movements. One of the more common ones sees the crucial predisposing factor as a social crisis, for example, cultural disintegration brought about by rapid change or contact with a foreign culture, especially if that culture seems superior. In its crude form, this type of theory assumes that some objective, massive dislocation in the sociohistorical situation is the virtual cause of the millenarian movement or apocalyptic mentality. In this form at least, such theories are clearly inadequate. Kenelm Burridge, an anthropologist who has written on millenarian movements, has pointed out repeatedly that the very same sociohistorical conditions sometimes are the occasion of an apocalyptic message and other times are not.[62] Many, if not all, apocalyptic texts can be understood as responses to crises; some of these are very specific sociopolitical situations (Daniel, 4 Ezra, 2 Baruch, Revelation) and others are more general, like the problem of death (the Testament of Abraham). But it is surely wrongheaded to give full or even primary explanatory power to these crises. In response to the destruction of Jerusalem, some Jews wrote apocalypses and others founded rabbinical schools. In circumstances similar to those in which John wrote his apocalypse, other Christians wrote letters advising obedience to the authorities (1 Peter) and still others wrote apologies for the Christian faith and way of life (Melito). Factors of background, temperament, and, to some degree, choice of theological perspective are crucial in differentiating one author from another. Such factors are at least as important as aspects of the sociohistorical situation in producing an apocalyptic mentality.

Another generalization about millenarianism and apocalypticism is that they are essentially the religious expression of "deprived" groups. One often hears that the author and first readers of Revelation were "oppressed." When social scientists use these terms they generally refer to groups that are in really extreme or dire circumstances, those threatened constantly by hunger, or suffering the consequences of famine, massive unemployment, plague, devastating fire, or other disasters. The theory is that the apocalyptic hope for the future is born out of abysmal despair. The vision of a new world is compensation for the miserable circumstances of the present. As soon as one asks whether this theoretical framework fits Revelation, one gets into difficulties. Were the complacent, wealthy members of the congregation in Laodicea oppressed? If Christians in Thyatira and Pergamum were despairing about the possibilities of the present, why did some of them turn to the teaching of the Nicolaitans, "Balaam," and "Jezebel"? One could say that the author himself and at least some readers were oppressed. Antipas was killed, John banished, some at Smyrna were threatened with arrest, and some in both Smyrna and Philadelphia were experiencing difficulties because of the ill will of some of their Jewish neighbors. But were these oppressed relative to some other groups in the empire? Were they as badly off as the slaves who worked the mines?

This type of question has led many social scientists to speak of "relative deprivation" rather than simply "deprivation" or "oppression." The predisposing factor in some millenarian movements has been seen in a marked disparity between expectations and their satisfaction. Sometimes a millenarian mentality arises because traditional expectations can no longer be met. The inability to meet traditional expectations has resulted from conditions like surplus population, a shift from rural to urban life, and industrialization. In other cases, it is a matter of the development of a new set of expectations without the establishment of means to achieve them. This situation has arisen when primitive societies first come into contact with modern ones. In the latter type of situation, frustration of new expectations is a more important factor than the simple lack of certain goods or abilities.

This last type of theory is illuminating for the Apocalypse. The response to elements of crisis and trauma reflects frustration. This frustration is not due to a recent encounter with a different culture perceived to be superior. Rather, it is due to the conflict between the Christian faith itself, as John understood it, and the social situation as he perceived it. A new set of expectations had arisen as a result of faith in Jesus as the Messiah and of belief that the kingdom of God and Christ had been established. It was the tension between John's vision of the kingdom of God and his environment that moved him to write his Apocalypse.

From this point of view, the book of Revelation is not simply a product of a certain social situation, not even a simple response to circumstances. At root is a particular religious view of reality, inherited in large part, which is the framework within which John interpreted his environment. The book of Revelation is thus a product of the interaction between a kind of pre-understanding and the sociohistorical situation in which John lived.

We will look at the literary function of Revelation from this point of view in Chapter 5. But first let us see how John responded to crisis and trauma on a social level. His response to rejection, suspicion, and repression on the part of outsiders was to call for a Christian communal life of social radicalism, as we will see in the next chapter.

NOTES

1. J. G. Gager, *Kingdom and Community: The Social World of Early Christianity* (Prentice-Hall, 1975), p. 27.

2. Wilhelm Bousset, *Die Offenbarung Johannis,* 5th ed. (Göttingen: Vandenhoeck & Ruprecht, 1896), pp. 242–243; R. H. Charles, *A Critical and Exegetical Commentary on the Revelation of St. John,* ICC (Charles Scribner's Sons, 1920), Vol. 1, pp. 56–58; J. A. T. Robinson, *Redating the New Testament* (Westminster Press, 1976), pp. 273–274. In support of the theory that the group referred to are local Jews, see Elisabeth Schüssler Fiorenza, "Apocalyptic and Gnosis in the Book of Revelation and Paul," *JBL* 92 (1973), p. 572.

3. G. E. M. de Ste. Croix, "Why Were the Early Christians Persecuted?" *Past and Present* 26 (1963).

4. Against Bousset (*Die Offenbarung Johannis,* pp. 278–279) and Charles (*A Critical and Exegetical Commentary on the Revelation of St. John,* Vol. 1, pp. 63, 69–70), who see the basic issue, but in too simple and narrow a perspective; in agreement with Ernst Lohmeyer (*Die Offenbarung des Johannes,* 2d ed.; Tübingen: J. C. B. Mohr [Paul Siebeck], 1953; p. 31) and G. B. Caird (*A Commentary on the Revelation of St. John the Divine;* Harper & Row, 1966; pp. 38–41, 44).

5. Rev. 17:2; 18:3, 9; *porneia* is used metaphorically in all but one of its occurrences outside the messages (14:8; 17:2, 4; 18:3; 19:2). In the one case in which it is probably used literally, *porneia* is associated with idolatry (9:20–21).

6. E.-B. Allo, *Saint Jean: L'Apocalypse,* 4th ed. (Paris: J. Gabalda, 1933), pp. 46–47; Charles, *A Critical and Exegetical Commentary on the Revelation of St. John,* Vol. 1, p. 69; I. T. Beckwith, *The Apocalypse of John* (Macmillan Co., 1919), pp. 463–464; William Ramsay,

The Letters to the Seven Churches of Asia (New York: Armstrong, 1905), pp. 316–353.

7. Beckwith, *The Apocalypse of John,* pp. 464–465.

8. Harald Fuchs, *Der geistige Widerstand gegen Rom in der antiken Welt* (Berlin: Walter de Gruyter, 1938).

9. The story is cited by Fuchs, ibid., pp. 5–7.

10. Ibid., pp. 5, 29n16.

11. Ibid., pp. 15, 44n44.

12. Ibid., pp. 16–17, 47n52.

13. Ibid., pp. 17, 47n53.

14. Ramsay MacMullen, *Enemies of the Roman Order* (Harvard University Press, 1966), pp. 148–149.

15. Ibid., p. 130.

16. The translation is by John J. Collins, "The Sibylline Oracles," in J. H. Charlesworth (ed.), *Old Testament Pseudepigrapha,* Vol. 1 (Doubleday & Co., 1983), p. 370.

17. Ibid., Introduction to Book 3.

18. Ibid., Introduction to Book 4.

19. David Magie, *Roman Rule in Asia Minor* (Princeton University Press, 1950), Vol. 1, p. 582.

20. T. R. S. Broughton, "Roman Asia," in Tenney Frank (ed.), *An Economic Survey of Ancient Rome* (Pageant Books, 1959), p. 4.

21. Collins, "The Sibylline Oracles," Introduction to Book 5.

22. Ibid., Introduction to Book 8.

23. M. Rostovtzeff, *The Social and Economic History of the Roman Empire* (Oxford: Clarendon Press, 1926), p. 111.

24. C. S. Walton, "Oriental Senators in the Service of Rome: A Study of Imperial Policy Down to the Death of Marcus Aurelius," *Journal of Roman Studies* 19 (1929), p. 51.

25. MacMullen, *Enemies of the Roman Order,* pp. 183–184; F. E. Peters, *The Harvest of Hellenism* (Simon & Schuster, 1970), pp. 525–526.

26. Plutarch *Moralia* 822A; cited by MacMullen, *Enemies of the Roman Order,* p. 183.

27. Magie, *Roman Rule in Asia Minor,* Vol. 1, p. 600.

28. MacMullen, *Enemies of the Roman Order,* pp. 183–184.

29. Magie, *Roman Rule in Asia Minor,* Vol. 1, p. 600.

30. Arnaldo Momigliano, "Sabinus (4), Titus Flavius," *OCD,* p. 786.

31. Karl Oscar Brink, "Dio (1), Cocceianus," *OCD,* p. 282.

32. Magie, *Roman Rule in Asia Minor,* Vol. 2, p. 1443n37.

33. Ibid., Vol. 1, p. 581.

34. Dio Chrysostom, *Orat.* 46.10–11; the translation is by H. Lamar Crosby in the LCL.

35. Ibid., 46.4.

36. Crosby, Introduction to the forty-seventh discourse, *Dio Chrysostom,* LCL, Vol. 4, pp. 243–245; Magie, *Roman Rule in Asia Minor,* Vol. 1, pp. 589–590.

37. E. A. Judge, *The Social Pattern of the Christian Groups in the First Century* (London: Tyndale Press, 1960), pp. 40–48.

38. Ibid., p. 41.

39. Pliny, *Letters* 10.33–34.

40. Ibid., 10.92–93.

41. Ibid., 10.96. See A. N. Sherwin-White, *Fifty Letters of Pliny* (London: Oxford University Press, 1967), pp. 176–177.

42. W. H. C. Frend, *Martyrdom and Persecution in the Early Church* (Oxford: Basil Blackwell, 1965), pp. 104–120, 163.

43. Ibid., pp. 162–163; Martin Dibelius, "Rom und die Christen im ersten Jahrhundert," *Botschaft und Geschichte. Gesammelte Aufsätze,* Vol. 2, *Zum Urchristentum und zur hellenistischen Religionsgeschichte* (Tübingen: J. C. B. Mohr [Paul Siebeck], 1956), pp. 208–211.

44. Frend, *Martyrdom and Persecution in the Early Church,* pp. 165–166.

45. Ibid., pp. 167–169.

46. Pliny, *Letters* 10.96–97.

47. Caird, *A Commentary on the Revelation of St. John the Divine,* pp. 37–38; Austin Farrer, *A Rebirth of Images: The Making of St. John's Apocalypse* (London: Dacre Press, 1949), pp. 190–191; A. N. Sherwin-White, *Roman Society and Roman Law in the New Testament* (Oxford: Clarendon Press, 1963), pp. 4–5, 8–11.

48. Tertullian, *De Praescr.* 36; Jerome, *De Vir. Ill.* 9.

49. Kleinfeller, "Relegatio," PW 2. IA. 564–565; Juvenal, *Sat.* 6. 553–564.

50. MacMullen, *Enemies of the Roman Order,* p. 126.

51. Ibid., p. 128.

52. Ibid., pp. 128–162, especially pp. 142–162.

53. Ibid., p. 130.

54. Pliny, *Letters* 10.56–57; Sherwin-White, *Roman Society and Roman Law in the New Testament,* p. 77.

55. Kleinfeller, "Deportatio in insulam," PW 5.231–233.

56. Cited by Caird, *A Commentary on the Revelation of St. John the Divine,* p. 21.

57. J. N. Sanders, "St. John on Patmos," *NTS* 9 (1963), pp. 76–77.

58. Victorinus, *In Apoc.* 10.11.

59. Cited by Eusebius, *Hist. Eccl.* 5.24.3; my thanks to Martin Hengel for calling this passage to my attention.

60. Sanders, "St. John on Patmos," p. 76.

61. Suetonius, *Augustus* 45 (implied), 65 (Postumus to Surrentum); *Tiberius* 50 (Julia to Rhegium).

62. Kenelm O. L. Burridge, "Reflections on Prophecy and Prophetic Groups," *Semeia* 21 (1981), pp. 99–100.

4

Social Radicalism
in the Apocalypse

In the last chapter we saw that elements of social crisis and individual and collective trauma are reflected in the book of Revelation. One aspect of the response taken and advocated by the author is a socially radical stance. John and his book were socially radical in a variety of ways. We have seen that he drew upon the anti-Roman stance of certain strata of subject eastern peoples, especially the form taken in the Jewish *Sibylline Oracles*. John adapted oral and literary anti-Roman tradition into a particularly fierce and dualistic literary image of the insurmountable opposition between the servants of God and the servants of Rome. He highlighted and emphasized the suffering of Christians at the hands of Rome and painted a picture of the empire which put this trait of persecutor at the very center. In this way he apparently hoped to reinforce whatever hostility to Rome his readers might already have had and to awaken an anti-Roman attitude in those who were neutral or even open to Roman culture. A close study of the function of the theme of persecution in the book is crucial to understanding how John viewed Rome and how the readers were encouraged to respond to the empire and its representatives.

THE THEME OF PERSECUTION

The book of Revelation is composed of two great cycles of visions, 1:9–11:19 and 12:1–22:5. Each of these cycles is made up of three series of seven: (1) seven each of messages, seals, and trumpets; (2) (seven) unnumbered visions, (seven) bowls, and another series of (seven) unnumbered visions. The structure of the book may be summarized as follows:

1. Prologue	1:1–8
Preface	1:1–3
Prescript and sayings	1:4–8
The seven messages	1:9–3:22
The seven seals	4:1–8:5
The seven trumpets	8:2–11:19
2. Seven unnumbered visions	12:1–15:4
The seven bowls	15:1–16:20
Babylon appendix	17:1–19:10
Seven unnumbered visions	19:11–21:8
Jerusalem appendix	21:9–22:5
Epilogue	22:6–21
Sayings	22:6–20
Benediction	22:21

Beginning with the seven seals, each series expresses the whole message of the book in its own particular way. The constant elements of the message are *(a)* persecution, *(b)* punishment of the persecutors, and *(c)* salvation of the persecuted.[1]

The first great cycle of visions introduced these elements in a way that seems to be purposefully veiled and fragmentary. The second cycle maintains the mythic and symbolic language of the first, but presents the underlying message of the book in a generally fuller and more coherent manner. In particular, the second cycle is more explicit about the historical contexts of the visions. The first cycle makes clear that persecution is of major importance, but it is only in the second cycle that the identity of the persecutors is made explicit, namely, the Roman authorities.

THE FIRST CYCLE OF VISIONS

The opening vision with its seven messages mentions two incidents of actual persecution and expresses the expectation of more. In 1:9, John refers to himself as "your partner in the tribulation . . . and endurance in Jesus." In themselves, tribulation *(thlipsis)* and endurance *(hypomonē)* are rather general terms. Their association with the kingdom (of God) and other aspects of the context suggest that they refer to the great crisis of the last days, which was often expected to involve persecution by those in power. In the same verse, John says that he was on the island of Patmos on account of the word of God and the testimony of Jesus. As we have seen, John's presence on Patmos was most probably due to Roman repression. Near the very beginning of the book, therefore, we find the theme of persecution and the Roman Empire linked implicitly.

The second clear case of persecution involves Antipas (2:13), whose death is mentioned in the message to Pergamum. As we have seen, various elements in the message suggest that Antipas was executed by the Roman governor because of his Christian faith. John's banishment and Antipas' death are clear examples of persecution, but they are spoken of in an indirect way. The first readers would have known of Roman responsibility for the incidents, but they are not invited to dwell on the fact.

The general tone of the messages implies that further persecution is expected. Emphasis is repeatedly placed on the quality of endurance or steadfastness *(hypomonē)*. In most cases the reference is not to a general characteristic of the life of faith, but to the stance to be taken in the context of persecution, which is seen as the tribulation of the last days. The Ephesians are praised for their endurance, exemplified in their bearing up "on account of my name" (2:3). The latter phrase indicates formal or informal interrogation with regard to Christian faith, and thus persecution or the pressure of public opinion. The expectation of further persecution is explicit in the message to Smyrna (2:10). Those faced with persecution are urged not to fear and to be faithful unto death. Similar exhortation is given in 2:13, 19, 25; 3:8, 10–11.

In the next series of seven, the seals, persecution is presented even more clearly as a major element in the events of the last days. When the fifth seal was opened, John saw under the (heavenly) altar the souls of those who had been slain on account of the word of God and the witness that they had held (6:9). They addressed the holy and true ruler saying, "How long until you will pass judgment and avenge our blood upon those who dwell upon the earth?" The association of the souls with the heavenly altar implies that their deaths are sacrifices offered to God.[2] The expectation that God would avenge innocent blood is attested elsewhere, as is the idea of a fixed number of souls who must go to their rest before the end could come.[3] What is distinctive about this passage is the combination of these elements. The result is the idea that there is a fixed number of persons who must die for their faith before the end can arrive, and that the catastrophe of the last days is vengeance on the adversaries of those who have died. From this point of view, the role of the saints is not purely passive; rather there is the possibility of a kind of synergism. Each death for the faith brings the end closer. In keeping with the presence of this vision in the first great cycle, the reader is not given any information about the specific circumstances of the deaths or the identity of the persecutors.

The vision containing the cry for vengeance is immediately followed by a proleptic description of the final battle against the kings of the earth (sixth seal). This sequence suggests that John viewed the battle of the end time as divine vengeance for the blood of those who died for their faith. This impression is strengthened by the vision that provides a transition from the seals to the trumpets (8:3–5). An angel stands at the (heavenly) altar with a golden censer, offering incense and the prayers of the saints to God. The altar is evidently the same one mentioned in the fifth seal. Here it is said to be a golden altar before the throne. Mention of the prayers of the saints and of the (heavenly) altar brings the vision of the fifth seal to mind with its prayer for vengeance. After offering the prayers, the angel takes fire from the altar and throws it upon the earth. This act suggests that the destruction that follows the trumpets is the divine answer to the prayer of the saints. Once again, no details are given about the opponents of the saints, and the destruction affects the whole earth. There is only a hint that the trumpets are directed against a particular group. The fifth trumpet is directed against people who lack the seal of God on their foreheads. Other passages imply that these are the followers of the beast; on one level of meaning, then, they are supporters of the Roman order (13:3–4, 8, 12–17; 17:8).[4]

In the first great cycle of visions, persecution is clearly an important element in the view of the end time presented by Revelation. There are hints about the nature of this persecution, but it is only in the second cycle that the Roman Empire is revealed as the proximate enemy of Christians.

THE SECOND CYCLE OF VISIONS

This cycle begins with a series of seven unnumbered visions (12:1–15:4). In this first series, the two persecuting beasts arise bearing unmistakable traits of Rome (13:1–18).[5] Later, three angels appear, each with a message. The second angel announces, "Fallen, fallen, is Babylon the great, who gave all the nations to drink of the wine of the wrath [or passion] of her harlotry" (14:8). As we have seen, "Babylon" is a "name of mystery" for Rome. The third angel proclaims, "If anyone worships the beast and his image . . . , he himself will also drink the wine of God's wrath . . . , and will be tortured with fire and brimstone before the holy angels and before the Lamb"

(14:9–11). This proclamation is addressed to the readers as a warning that collaboration with the Roman Empire and submission to its claims will lead to eternal damnation. This function is confirmed by the remark that follows, "Here is the endurance of the saints, who keep the commandments of God and the faith of Jesus" (14:12).

The climactic vision of salvation in 15:2–4 completes the series. It is interlocked with the opening vision of the next series, the seven bowls.[6] Like the seals and trumpets, the bowls are universal and cosmic in their effects. The trumpets, as noted above, contain a hint that they are directed against a particular group (9:4). It was also noted that the trumpets are presented as the answer to the prayer of the saints for vengeance. These two elements are also present in the bowls. The third bowl has a distinctive commentary that designates that particular plague as a punishment on those who have shed the blood of the saints (16:5–7).[7] The persecutors are not explicitly identified in the third bowl, but the context suggests who they are. The first and fifth bowls are directed against the beast and its followers. As we have seen, the beast, on one level of meaning, represents Rome. The bowls are introduced as the result of God's wrath (15:1). One of the effects of the seventh bowl is the fall of Babylon, which is explicitly attributed to the wrath of God (16:19). This statement recalls the opening remark and shows that the fall of Babylon is the climax of the seven bowls. The implication is that the plagues of the seven bowls are God's judgment on the whole earth for its complicity in Rome's persecution of the people of God.

The background against which this idea must be understood is the sense that there is some sort of solidarity between human behavior and the natural world. This sense is expressed in various biblical and Hellenistic texts. According to the *Kore Kosmou*, a text in the Egyptian Hermetic collection, the four natural elements are polluted by human actions, especially murder.[8] In Genesis, Adam is told: "Cursed is the ground because of you" (3:17). Paul also thought within this framework (Rom. 8:19–23). According to Isaiah 24, human sin brings divine wrath on the natural world as well as on humanity (vs. 1–7); it puts the covenant curses into effect.

In the *Kore Kosmou*, the perception that there is something deeply wrong with the world is expressed in the image of the pollution of the elements at the beginning of time. The righting of this state of affairs is accomplished by the activities of the saving figures Osiris and Isis, who put the lower realm in harmony with the upper realm by means of civilization and cult. The idea that something is radically amiss in the world is expressed in Revelation also. But the "something" in

Revelation is not the human propensity to violence or human sin in general. It is the persecution of Christians by Rome, past and expected, real and imagined.

The persecution envisioned in Revelation is not to be halted in a way similar to the cessation of murder in the *Kore Kosmou.* In the latter text, the punishment of guilty individuals—both living and dead —is to be a deterrent to further violence and the envisaged result is a universe of order and justice. In Revelation the magnitude of the disorder can be righted only by the destruction of the world as it had been known and by the creation of a "new heaven and a new earth" (21:1) that have little in common with this world (21:4, 23; 22:5).

ATTITUDE TOWARD THE PERSECUTORS

Revelation 17 and 18 elaborate the judgment of Babylon announced in 16:19, and 19:1–10 presents heavenly rejoicing over the fulfillment of that judgment. Chapter 18 is a powerful passage, although its effect is somewhat ambiguous. The current consensus among commentators is that the chapter depicts the destruction of the city of Rome and the breakdown of the world order associated with it.[9] Opinions differ on the function of the passage and on the attitude of the author to the catastrophe he portrays. A number of interpreters argue that it expresses joy in the triumph of God's cause and not a personal desire for revenge.[10] Others assume that hatred or personal vindictiveness is at least one element that motivated the composition of Revelation 18 or even of the book as a whole.[11] In sharp contrast to those who find the passage vengeful, others detect elements of real pathos, awe, and even regret at the fall of Rome.[12]

LITERARY FORMS IN REVELATION 18

Decisions about the function of ch. 18 should be based on careful analysis of the literary form and function of the constituent units. At first glance, the passage seems to be a rather loose grouping of a variety of forms. A closer look shows that a number of small units are joined into three main sections: (1) a report of a vision (vs. 1–3), (2) a report of an audition (vs. 4–20), and (3) a narrative account of a symbolic action performed by an angel (vs. 21–24).

The opening vision is of an angel coming down from heaven. Most of the section is a report of the angel's words (vs. 2b–3). In terms of form, the angel's speech is a dirge spoken over Babylon. Originally, the dirge was a form of oral folk literature, a lament spoken over a corpse. The form had other functions, some of which were metaphorical.[13] The prophets sometimes used the dirge as a vivid announcement of judgment, sometimes on Israel, sometimes on its enemies.[14] The angel's dirge in Rev. 18:2–3 has as its function the announcement of judgment on an enemy; v. 2b is the actual announcement; and v. 3 gives the grounds for the judgment.

The second major section is the most diverse in form and content. Commentators disagree on the extent of the report of the words of the heavenly voice. Some do not consider it to continue through v. 20, but hold that there is a shift from a report to the words of the author himself. There is disagreement, however, on where the shift occurs. Since there is no clear indication in the text of a change of speaker, it seems best to include all of vs. 4–20 in the heavenly speech. This speech contains a number of smaller units that can be distinguished by shifts in one or more of the following characteristics: addressee, grammatical mood, person, tense, and function. These shifts justify distinctions in literary form.

The first such unit is an admonition (vs. 4b–5) that begins, "Come out of her, my people." The phrase "my people" seems to imply that God is the speaker, but the conclusion is "God has remembered her iniquities." The two parts of the saying clearly belong together, since v. 4b is the actual warning and v. 5 gives the reasons for it. A number of commentators conclude that Christ is the speaker. But the opening remark is a scriptural allusion (Jer. 51:45), so it is best to assume that the speaker is an angel or to leave the speaker unspecified.

Verses 6–8 constitute the second small unit, which is a command to execute judgment upon Babylon. The speaker and the addressee are not explicitly identified. Parallels in Ezekiel show that the speaker may be an angel or God and that the addressees are probably heavenly beings (Ezek. 9:1, 5–6). Like the dirge of vs. 2b–3 and the admonition of vs. 4b–5, this speech falls into two parts. The actual commands are given in vs. 6–7a and the explanation is given in vs. 7b–8. There is some overlap of the two elements, however, because of the use of the principle of correlation. For example, the command to give to her as she herself gave (to others) implies that her previous behavior called for divine judgment: the punishment fits the crime. Besides that direct kind of correlation, an antithetical parallelism between deed and punishment is made. Her torment and degradation will be in proportion to her self-glorification.

The third small unit is an announcement of judgment in vs. 9–10. It is directed against the kings of the earth and foretells their fear and distress at Babylon's fall. The announcement includes a dirge spoken by the kings over the city. On one level of meaning, within the immediate literary context, and from the perspective of the speakers, the dirge is a real, though metaphorical, one. It expresses genuine distress on the part of Rome's friends. In the book as a whole, and from the perspective of the author and intended readers, however, the dirge functions as an announcement of judgment in the same way as the angel's dirge of verses 2b–3. This function is made clear in the wording of the dirge, "In one hour your *judgment* has come" (emphasis added).

A number of commentators take vs. 11–17a together as a unit and describe it as the dirge or lament of the merchants. Some of these and other commentators consider v. 14 to be displaced and transpose it to a position within vs. 21–24. There is no textual evidence to indicate that v. 14 is misplaced. In view of the lack of such evidence, the interpreter should first ask whether the verse is intelligible in its present location. Given the shift from third to second person, v. 14 should be taken as a unit distinct from what precedes and follows. Such an abrupt digression is not unique in the book of Revelation. The sayings in 13:9–10, 18; 14:12; and 16:15 are analogous. It seems most accurate, therefore, to distinguish vs. 11–13, 14, and 15–17a as the fourth, fifth, and sixth small units within the speech from heaven (vs. 4–20).

The fourth unit (vs. 11–13) is an announcement of judgment directed against the merchants of the earth. It differs from the announcement against the kings (vs. 9–10) in that it does not foretell their distress, but announces it in the present tense: "And the merchants of the earth weep and mourn over her" (v. 11a). The reason for their distress is given: "because no one buys their cargo any more" (vs. 11b–13). No dirge is quoted in this unit.

Verse 14, the fifth unit of the audition, is a dirge addressed to Babylon directly. The speaker is unspecified. The first two lines of the dirge are in the aorist tense: "And the fruit for which your soul longed has departed from you and all richness and splendor have perished from you." The use of the aorist is in keeping with the form; it appears also in the opening dirge and in that of the kings. The dirge of v. 14 closes with a prediction, "And they will surely not be found any more." Such a prediction is not necessarily out of place in an expression of mourning; nevertheless, the empathic denial with *ou mē* does point to the actual function of the dirge, the announcement of judgment.

The sixth small unit in this middle section is another announcement of judgment against the merchants (vs. 15–17a). This announcement is parallel in structure to that against the kings (vs. 9–10). It foretells the merchants' fear and distress at Babylon's fall and includes their dirge over the city. Here also, the dirge is a genuine one within the immediate literary context. There is no explicit indication in the wording that it is anything other than an expression of mourning. For that reason, some interpreters have inferred an attitude of awe, even a touch of sorrow, on the author's part. The parallel between this passage and the one about the kings makes such an attitude improbable. The kings are characterized in a highly negative way (v. 9) and their dirge characterizes Babylon's fall as her judgment. The parallelism between the kings and the merchants makes it unlikely that the author sympathized with their mourning or regretted the loss of their great wealth. Other indications support this hypothesis, as we shall see below.

The seventh small unit within the speech of the heavenly voice is another announcement of judgment, this time upon those who make their living from the sea (vs. 17b–19). The announcement against the kings (vs. 9–10) and the second announcement against the merchants (vs. 15–17a) are true to form in that they are in the future tense, as is expected. The first announcement against the merchants (vs. 11–13), as noted above, is in the present tense. The result is that the event seems more real, more immediate to the reader. The announcement against the mariners is in the past tense (aorist and imperfect). It is probable that the form of the vision account, so frequent in Revelation, has influenced this unit. In the account of a vision, the past tense is used to report what was seen in the past (see 18:1). The relation of the content of the vision to the ordinary sequence of events in reality must be inferred by the reader. The use of the past tense in the announcement against the mariners gives it less of an oracular, predictive character, and makes a more descriptive, narrative impression. Two dirges are quoted (vs. 18b, 19b). These dirges are genuine within the immediate literary context. There is no explicit indication within this passage of the author's attitude or the response the readers are intended to have. Like the dirge spoken by the merchants, this one emphasizes the wealth of Rome and of certain groups who profited by it. This announcement is also parallel to the one against the kings. That parallelism is an indication that the dirge is not intended to evoke sympathy.

The eighth and last unit in the audition report is the call for rejoicing in v. 20. It is similar in form to 12:12, where the heavens and those dwelling in them are urged to rejoice. Apparently by analogy with that verse, a number of commentators argue that the three groups mentioned here are heavenly dwellers. The reason for rejoicing is given in v. 20b in terse and ambiguous form. The language is legal and it is likely that John has in mind some who have actually been tried and executed by Roman authorities (see v. 24 and 2:13). It is not necessarily the case, however, that the call is addressed only to them.

The third major section of Revelation 18 is a narrative account of a symbolic action performed by an angel (vs. 21–24). There are some similarities between this passage and the accounts of a symbolic act in the Israelite prophets. In both cases one finds the report of the act and a statement of the meaning of the act. The major difference is that in the Jewish Bible a prophet performs the deed, whereas here an angel does so. Rev. 18:21–24 lacks the formulae that usually introduce accounts of visions and auditions, but they are surely implied.

The statement of the meaning of the act is an announcement of judgment on Babylon (vs. 21b–24). The first part of the statement, beginning "so, with a rush, will Babylon, the great city, be thrown down," is the actual explanation of the sign (v. 21b). It refers to Babylon in the third person. The second part is an elaboration addressed to Babylon in the second person (vs. 22–24). The address to Babylon closes with two reasons for the judgment against her: "because your merchants were the great ones of the earth, because all the nations were deceived by your sorcery" (v. 23cd). These reasons introduce two motifs that are new in the context of chs. 17–18; how they relate to reasons given elsewhere in these chapters will be discussed below. The third and last part of the announcement against Babylon is a simple statement in the third person: "and in her was found blood of prophets and saints and of all the slaughtered upon the earth." The context implies that this statement is a further reason for the judgment against Babylon. The shift to the third person gives it special emphasis.

Revelation 19:1 introduces a new audition, the voice, as it were, of a great crowd in heaven. This audition expresses the element of salvation or triumph, which follows that of punishment or judgment in chs. 17–18. Verse 20 of ch. 18 prepares for the transition in the familiar interlocking technique.

Two literary forms dominate Revelation 18, the announcement of judgment and the dirge. From the perspective of the author and the larger literary context, the dirges also function as announcements of judgment. The analysis of the dirges in Revelation 18 has shown that there is no simple, one-to-one correspondence in their case between form and function. On the surface, they express mourning. But when they function on another level to announce judgment, and when that judgment is on an enemy, the dirge takes on a paradoxical or ironic character, because of the unlikelihood of genuine mourning. Whether that irony is malicious is another question. The images used to portray Rome and the reasons given for its impending judgment have a significant bearing on the nature of the irony involved.

THE PORTRAYAL OF ROME IN REVELATION 17–18

One of the most prominent images in these two chapters is the name "Babylon." As we have seen, it is a portrayal of Rome as the (second) destroyer of Jerusalem. The use of this image in chs. 17–18 implies that the imminent downfall of Rome is viewed by the author, at least in part, as retribution for the destruction of Jerusalem.

Another prominent and striking image is Rome as a harlot visited by the kings of the earth (17:1–2; 18:3, 9; 19:2). The harlot image was applied by the prophets both to the people of God (Hos. 4:12–18; Isa. 1:21; Jer. 3:3–10; Ezek. 16:15–58; 23:1–49) and to their enemies (Nahum 3:4; Isa. 23:15–18). When applied to the people of God, the image is related to foreign alliances and cultic practices.[15] In Nahum 3:4, Nineveh is called a harlot who betrays peoples with her sorceries. In Isa. 23:15–18 the harlotry of Tyre is related to commerce. Most of these connotations seem to be intended in Revelation 17–18. The reference to blasphemous names (17:3), and possibly to abominations and impurities (17:4) also, alludes to improper cultic titles and practices. The allusion is probably to the imperial cult, which often included the worship of the goddess Roma. In Jewish ethics, harlotry, idolatry, and sorcery were often linked.[16] Sorcery is associated with Rome in 18:23. No explicit link is made between harlotry and commerce, but they are associated in the overall context.

In 17:2 it is said that those who dwell on earth have become drunk with the wine of her harlotry. This image must be understood on two levels. The first is suggested by the immediate context and the traditional connotations of harlotry; that is, all humanity have joined in her idolatrous worship. This meaning has a parallel in 18:23—all the nations were deceived by her sorcery. Involvement with Roman commerce may also be linked indirectly with this "drunkenness" by the parallel statements within 18:3 and 23, respectively. The second level of meaning is suggested by the parallel between "of the wine of her harlotry" (17:2) and "of the wine of the wrath [or passion] of her harlotry" (14:8 and 18:3). The phrase of 14:8 and 18:3 links the image of the wine of harlotry (17:2) with the image of the wine of the wrath of God (16:19 and 14:10). Thus, on another level, Babylon's "wine"

represents Rome as the conqueror of the earth. Rome's military victories are seen as part of God's plan (compare Jer. 51:7–8). Nevertheless, she will be punished for the blood she has shed (17:6; 18:24;
compare Jer. 51:49). Rome is criticized not only for persecuting Christians but on behalf of all who have been slain on earth. The repression
of the Jewish rebellion of 66–72 C.E. is probably alluded to here, and
perhaps also the subjugation of other peoples. The references to Babylon mixing a cup and rendering (to others), and to her "works" (18:6),
should probably be understood as further allusions to her military
victories and related violent deeds.

Another traditional element in the negative portrayal of Rome is
her self-glorification and arrogance (18:7). Such an attitude in Israel
and Judah and their enemies was often condemned by the prophets,
and the motif appears in intertestamental literature as well.[17] The
speech attributed to Babylon here is based on Isa. 47:7–8. The application of this traditional motif to Rome was probably a response to
Roman propaganda regarding the eternity and universality of Roman
dominance.[18]

All the images examined thus far not only describe Rome but give
reasons for her predicted downfall. The same seems to be true of the
depiction of Rome as wealthy (17:4; 18:16) and as a source of wealth
for merchants (18:3, 15) and shipowners (18:19). The merchants'
wealth is one of the reasons given for the judgment against Babylon
announced in the opening dirge (v. 3). That explanation has a parallel
in the closing scene: The first reason given by the angel with the great
stone for Babylon's demise is that her merchants were the great ones
of the earth (18:23). This theme of wealth as an occasion for judgment
has parallels in the oracles against Tyre in Isa. 23:1–12 and Ezek.
26:1–28:19. In these passages, economic wealth and blasphemous
pride are linked. Neither pity nor malicious joy is prominent. Rather,
wealth is seen as the occasion for an arrogant attitude and unrighteous
deeds. The oracles express the conviction that God brings down the
haughty and the unrighteous.

The attitude toward wealth in Revelation is more complex. A link
between wealth and arrogance seems to be implied by the criticism of
the Christians at Laodicea: "You say, 'I am rich and I have prospered
and I am in need of nothing,' and you do not know that you are
wretched" (3:17). Such a link may also be inferred from the similarity
between the description of the woman Babylon in luxurious attire and
her arrogant speech (compare 17:4 and 18:16 with 18:7–8). There are
indications, however, that wealth is viewed primarily from a more
social and political perspective in Revelation. As we have seen, the

anti-Romanism of Revelation stands in the tradition of anti-Roman propaganda among the subject peoples, especially in the East. We have also seen evidence of social unrest in Asia Minor around the end of the first century C.E. Even though much of the wording of Revelation 18 reflects Isaiah, Jeremiah, and Ezekiel, it is still likely that the passage reflects the social situation of Asia Minor in John's time.

In Revelation 18 we find judgment announced not only against Rome but also against wholesale dealers, shipmasters, and all whose livelihood comes from the sea. John probably had in mind here citizens of the cities of western Asia Minor who had amassed great wealth from commerce and the transportation of goods. Mikhail Rostovtzeff speaks of a new class of wealthy provincials who made their fortunes in this way under the Flavians.[19] In Revelation 18 their economic ruin is described and then heaven, saints, apostles, and prophets are called upon to rejoice. One important reason for this response was probably the feeling of being an outsider, the lack of any feeling of identification with or sympathy for the provincial elite or even the cities that they led. The combination of hostility toward the local elite and toward the Roman authorities is not surprising, since they cooperated with and supported one another; opposition to one could easily lead to or be associated with hostility to the other.[20]

The images of Rome as the new Babylon and the mother of harlots are hardly intended to evoke respect for the Roman Empire or regret at its fall. The reasons for Rome's judgment are clearly presented and unlikely to evoke sympathy or pathos. They may be summarized as follows: (1) the idolatrous and blasphemous worship offered and encouraged by Rome, especially the emperor cult; (2) the violence perpetrated by Rome, especially against Jews and Christians; (3) Rome's blasphemous self-glorification; and (4) Roman wealth. As we saw in Chapter 3, there were other, implicit reasons for John's opposition to Rome.

The various literary forms in Revelation 18 are united in the basic function of announcing divine judgment on "Babylon" and giving the reasons for it. The dirge is a prominent form in the chapter, and the relation between its form and function is complex and ambiguous. The dirges of the unspecified speaker (v. 14), the merchants (vs. 16–17a), and the mariners (vs. 18b–19) do not contain any obvious condemnations. When read in isolation, the traditional function of mourning is prominent. Such a reading could evoke sympathetic awe. The context shows, however, that if such pathos was intended by the author, it was primarily for dramatic effect. The parallelism among the kings, the merchants, and the mariners implies that all the misfortunes described, and not just those of the kings, are richly deserved punishments. Further, the powerful scenes of mourning are suddenly cut off by the call for rejoicing in v. 20. The position of this verse gives it a climactic character and implies that the primary response to the fall of Rome by the readers should be rejoicing, not regret. The mourning expressed by the dirges is strictly that of Babylon's friends. The conclusion that the dirges express no sympathy or regret on the part of the author is supported by the choice of images for Rome in chs. 17–18 and by the reasons given for the divine judgment of "Babylon."

As we saw in Chapter 3, the public identity of Christians in Asia Minor in John's time was precarious. The explicit, extreme, even abusive anti-Romanism of the book of Revelation could have made their status only more threatened. The literary attack on Rome is the most basic element of social radicalism in the Apocalypse. It is sometimes argued that symbols and coded language were used in Revelation so that the criticism of Rome could be kept secret from outsiders and the wrath of the Roman authorities avoided. This theory is not persuasive. Symbolic language was used more likely because of its intrinsic evocative power. In any case, it provides only the thinnest disguise, through which Rome is clearly recognizable. Any reader in the Mediterranean world in John's time, when reading the words, "And authority was given it over every tribe and people and tongue and nation, and all who dwell on earth will worship it" (13:7–8), would think of Rome. Other allusions, such as the mention of seven mountains in 17:9, are equally transparent. Further, the overall tone of Revelation suggests that John would rather have seen conflict between Rome and Christians intensified than abated. This tone is expressed in other forms of social radicalism.

CHRISTIAN EXCLUSIVISM

As we saw in Chapter 3, John's attacks on the Nicolaitans, "Balaam," and "Jezebel" show that he opposed participation by Christians in the civic life of Asia Minor and any significant cultural assimilation or even accommodation. His strict position on eating meat sacrificed to idols and his denunciation of "harlotry," that is, syncretism or perhaps even a mild religious tolerance, make it plain that he was calling upon Christians to avoid membership in guilds or other Gentile associations. The Christian fellowship alone could demand loyalty.

Another passage supports the idea that John was advocating social, political, and economic withdrawal from the life of the cities of western Asia Minor. Chapter 13 contains visions of a beast from the sea and a beast from the land. Here we have the same association of hostility to Rome (the beast from the sea) with hostility to the provincial elite (the beast from the land) that we found in ch. 18. The beast from the land is characterized as holding authority with permission of the first beast and as causing people to worship it. Members of the socially prominent and wealthy families of the region were those who held political office with Roman oversight and who held the various priesthoods, including that of the imperial ruler cult.

In 13:16–17 it is said of the beast from the land:

> And he causes all, the small and the great, and the rich and the poor, and the free and the slave, to be marked on the right hand or on the forehead,
>
> and [he brings it about] that no one is able to buy or sell unless he has the mark, the name of the beast, or the number of his name.

Giving those loyal to the beast a mark is a parody of the sealing of the elect, which is described in 7:1–8. The seal *(sphragis)* of the living God (7:2) is a guarantee of protection from the natural and demonic plagues of the end time (3:10; 7:3; 9:4), whereas the mark *(charagma)* of the beast marks its bearers for such plagues (16:2) and for eternal punishment (14:9–11). This idea of a mark or seal that determines one's fate is clearly traditional and reflects Ezekiel 9 and possibly *Pss. Sol.* 15:9–10. But it is also apparent that in painting this image, the author of Revelation made use of certain elements that had contemporary cultural associations and thus enhanced the effect of the image. The choice of the term *charagma,* for example, is significant since it was the technical term for the imperial stamp.[21] The idea of a mark or seal that determines one's fate was traditionally thought of as a mark on the forehead. The addition in our text of a reference to the right hand may be a parodying allusion to the Jewish practice of wearing phylacteries on the forehead and left hand or arm. The inversion from the left to the right hand is presumably part of the parody.[22] This nuance would fit the general theme of the book whereby the beast and his followers parody the Lamb and his followers, since the title "Jew" is claimed for followers of Jesus (2:9 and 3:9).

Verse 16 thus contains two probable allusions to the current historical situation. It is a matter of debate whether v. 17 also contains a contemporary reference. Wilhelm Bousset argued that v. 17 reflects a widespread mythic motif about the signs of the Antichrist, according to which only those sealed by the Antichrist are allowed to buy (and sell).[23] The use of a traditional motif is not incompatible with allusion to the contemporary historical situation, as was noted above in the discussion of v. 16. Thus, even if v. 17 does reflect a mythic motif, we should still ask how the image may have been shaped by the situation of the author.

It is unlikely that the inability to buy or sell refers to "a ruthless economic warfare" waged by the state against the elect, as R. H. Charles argued.[24] G. B. Caird rightly pointed out that John was probably aware that Roman hostility to non-Roman religious practice did not normally take the form of economic sanctions.[25] It seems rather that the juxtaposition of buying and selling with the mark of the beast refers to the fact that Roman coins normally bore the image and name of the current emperor. The inability to buy or sell would then be the result of the refusal to use Roman coins. Such a refusal is analogous to the Zealot refusal to carry, look at, or manufacture coins bearing any sort of image.[26] The explicit reason given for the Zealot refusal is a strict interpretation of the law against images. If John the prophet was a native of Palestine, or at least lived there for an extended period, as was argued in Chapter 1, he would have had opportunity to become familiar with the ideas of the Zealots and other opponents of Rome.

Judas the Galilean, one of the forerunners of the group who later called themselves Zealots, taught, on the basis of the First Commandment, that no one but God could be honored as "king" or "lord." Therefore, no foreigner could rule over Israel. Paying taxes to the emperor was a recognition of foreign rule and thus apostasy. The question put to Jesus in Mark 12:13-17 and parallels—"Is it lawful to pay taxes to Caesar, or not?"—reflects the debate instigated by Judas. Jesus' response implies that whoever participates in the Roman economic system by using Roman coins is bound to pay the tax; it is Caesar's due. Those who accepted Rome as the political authority ordained by God would thus read the story as a legitimation of limited cooperation with Rome and of the practice of paying taxes. The story and the saying of Jesus with which it culminates could be read quite differently, however, by those who saw Rome as a rebellious and blasphemous power analogous to the reign of Antiochus Epiphanes. In such a context the images and inscriptions of Roman coins would be idolatrous and thus contact with them was to be avoided. The relevant saying of Jesus would then have been read dualistically and as a mandate for separatism and possibly even economic boycott.[27] Evidently John was calling upon his readers to avoid using the coin of the realm. Such avoidance would have implied economic separatism of some sort. This call was reinforced by the proclamation of the third angel in ch. 14:

> If any one worships the beast and its image, and receives a mark on his forehead or on his hand, he also shall drink the wine of God's wrath, . . . and he shall be tormented with fire and brimstone in the presence of the holy angels and in the presence of the Lamb. And the smoke of their torment goes up for ever and ever; and they have no rest, day or night, these worshipers of the beast and its image, *and whoever receives the mark of its name.* (14:9–11; emphasis added)

In ch. 18 a heavenly voice calls out:

> Come out of her my people, lest you take part in her sins, lest you share in her plagues; for her sins are heaped high as heaven, and God has remembered her iniquities. (18:4–5)

This call apparently was not a summons to avoid corruption by retreating to the desert, as the Essene community at Qumran did. The flight of the woman to the wilderness (12:6, 14) is sometimes understood as a literal, physical withdrawal of the Christian community. In the light of John's polemic against the Nicolaitans, "Balaam," and "Jezebel" in the seven messages, and of the indirect exhortation to economic separatism in 13:17, it is more likely that he was calling for social exclusivism than physical removal.

MARTYRDOM AND VIRGINITY

Further evidence of the social radicalism of the author is found in 14:1–5, a vision of the Lamb on Mt. Zion, "and with him a hundred and forty-four thousand who had his name and his Father's name written on their foreheads." This group is apparently the same as those sealed on their foreheads in 7:1–8. Several elements suggest that the 144,000 are a special group within the body of the saints and not Christians in general. First of all, they are numbered. This fact distinguishes them from the innumerable multitude described in 7:9–17, who are all the faithful. The probable symbolic character of the number 144,000 is not incompatible with the suggestion of a limited group. It is said that they sing a new song before the throne and before the four living creatures and before the elders. The song is not quoted; in fact, it is said that no one could learn this song except the 144,000 who had been redeemed from the earth (v. 3). This song, known only to them, suggests that they are an exclusive group.

They are also described as "firstfruits" from humankind who have been redeemed for God and the Lamb. The image of the firstfruits distinguishes them from the general harvest of the faithful. The phrase suggests both an untimely and violent death—they are offered to God as a sacrifice—and also that they take part in the first resurrection, the general resurrection being the "harvest" (see 20:13). The idea of their untimely and violent deaths, presumably for their faith in Christ, is reinforced by the phrase "It is these who follow the Lamb wherever he goes" (14:4)—that is, even unto death, a death like that of the cross.

The suggestion that they take part in the first resurrection is confirmed by the vision of the messianic reign:

> And I saw thrones, and they sat upon them, and judgment was given to them, and [I saw] the souls of those who had been beheaded on account of the witness of Jesus and the word of God, and who [or whoever] did not worship the beast or his image and did not receive the mark on the forehead and on the hand. They came to life and reigned with Christ a thousand years. (20:4)

The text is ambiguous on the issue of participation in this messianic reign. If the relative pronoun *(hoitines)* retains its classical sense (whoever), it would refer to a wider circle than those beheaded for the faith. Thus participation would seem to be open to all faithful Christians. But *hoitines* in New Testament Greek most often functions just like the ordinary relative.[28] As we have seen, John's Greek is hardly shaped by classical models. Thus the relative clause may be a further qualification of "the souls of those who had been beheaded," namely, those who did not worship the beast, etc. If the relative clause is a further qualification, then participation would be limited to those who had died for the faith. The argument that the relative clause refers at least in part to Christians still living is weak because it necessitates reading the verb "they came to life" in two different senses simultaneously. Furthermore, the reference to "the rest of the dead" in v. 5 implies that those mentioned just previously were also dead in the usual sense. It is thus likely that the messianic reign was limited in John's mind to those who had died for the faith. At least it is clear that they were singled out for special emphasis. The first resurrection and the exercise of kingly power with Christ are blessings by which those who share the fate of Jesus with regard to his death are also enabled to share in his glorious destiny.

As we saw earlier in this chapter, the vision of the fifth seal suggests that every death for the faith brings the end closer. The visions of the

144,000 and the messianic reign show that such a death is a way of following the Lamb that is specially valued by God and will be specially rewarded. This stance of openness to violent death is another way in which the book of Revelation is socially radical. The willingness to die made it possible to criticize Rome and the cultural values of the time.

One of the striking characteristics of the 144,000 is that they "have not defiled themselves with women, for they are virgins" (14:4). Some interpreters take these words metaphorically, arguing that the sexual language here is analogous to John's use of the term "harlotry," which, as we have seen, often meant idolatry (2:14; 17:2). It is more likely that actual sexual practice is meant in 14:4, because of the concreteness and specificity of the terms used. Even though there is no other reference to sexual continence in Revelation, it is likely that John is presenting it here as a quality of the ideal Christian life.

It is improbable that John had lifelong celibacy in mind, a value and practice that did not become normative for men in the early church until several centuries later. His words probably refer to continence during the latter part of one's life. Philo, a Greek-speaking Jew of Alexandria who lived in the first centuries B.C.E. and C.E., says that the Essenes of Palestine banned marriage and ordered the practice of perfect continence among themselves.[29] He also says that there were no children, or even adolescents or young men, among them, but that the members of their associations were "men of ripe years already inclining to old age."[30] Flavius Josephus, a Jew from Palestine who wrote in Greek, says in one place that the Essenes did not themselves marry, but did not seek to abolish marriage and the propagation of the human race. Later in the same account, he says that there were two orders of Essenes, one that married and had children, and another that did not.[31]

The Essene documents themselves suggest that some of them did marry. The Damascus Document says, "And if they live in camps according to the rule of the Land (or as it was from ancient times), marrying . . . and begetting children, they shall walk according to the law."[32] The Annex to the Community Rule mentions women and children as part of the congregation and contains provisions for sexual intercourse, presumably within marriage.[33] The archaeological data, however, suggest that the Essene community at Qumran was largely celibate. The large central cemetery there seems to have contained only burials of men. Skeletons of women and children have been found in outlying cemeteries.[34]

The evidence is ambiguous, but two things are clear: the Essenes did not have a well-developed teaching in favor of lifelong celibacy; nevertheless, there was a tendency toward valuing continence. The evidence can be explained in at least two ways: (1) there were two orders of Essenes; one included marriage, the other was characterized by continence; (2) Essenes married and begot children in their youth; at a certain age they became continent for the remainder of their lives. The Essene tendency toward continence seems to have several roots.[35] One root is the ancient set of ideas and practices related to purity in Israel. Sexual intercourse was thought of as defiling. It was not forbidden, wrong, or sinful, but it made a person unfit to come in contact with the sacred until purified. The regulations about purity were especially important for priests, who had to come in touch with the sacred regularly and in special ways. It is significant in this regard that the leaders at Qumran were priests.

A second, related root is the mentality and practice of holy war. The early Israelites believed that Yahweh and his angels were present in their military camps and fought alongside them. Because of this sacred presence these camps had to be especially pure. All sexual activities were suspended and special sanitary regulations were in force. For at least one order of Essenes, the priestly purity regulations and the rules of holy war became a way of life. The reason is that they considered themselves to be living in the last days and tried to prepare themselves for the final battle of the end time, which they saw in terms of holy war.

The selection of continence as an aspect of ideal Christian life in the Apocalypse seems to have a similar logic to that of the Essenes. Although there is no sign that John expected Christians to fight in the great battle of the end time, his vision of the battle itself is shaped by holy war tradition. In Rev. 19:11–21, Christ is presented as the divine warrior who does battle on behalf of his people and defeats their adversaries. The mythic pattern of combat, which is used often in the Jewish Bible to portray Yahweh as the divine warrior, is the basic principle of composition in the Apocalypse.[36] Thus, the struggle with Rome was interpreted by John as a holy war. Even if Christians were not to fight, they could still do their part by remaining pure and ready to die.

Further, John believed that all Christians were priests. By his blood Jesus "made us a kingdom, priests to his God and Father" (1:6). The same point is made in 5:10. There is no indication that John taught that Christians as priests should observe ritual washings or other rites associated with purity. But the practice of continence may well have symbolized for him the purity to which the Christian priest is called. If John was a native of Palestine or lived there for an extended period, he would undoubtedly have been familiar with the practices and ideas of the Essenes. Their thinking may have influenced him on this issue.

It is striking that the value of continence is expressed in Rev. 14:4 from an exclusively male point of view. The reason for this could be John's patriarchal point of view, which he inherited. If we are correct, however, in concluding that priesthood and holy war provide the background for his view on continence, the male point of view is even more intelligible. Warriors and priests, especially in Jewish tradition, were generally men.

In any case, continence was valued by many in the early church. First Corinthians 7 shows that Paul held the continent single state to be the best way of life under the circumstances. Given that Christians were living in the last days, sexual relations, marriage, family life, and all that went with them were seen primarily as distractions from the major task of preparation for the end. Paul took a moderate position, however, because he realized that such a life-style was not appropriate for everyone, even in the last days. He opposed some Corinthians who were practicing continence within marriage, a way of life that became very common in the early church later on. The Gospel of Matthew presents Jesus teaching that some are called to make themselves eunuchs for the kingdom of heaven (Matt. 19:10–12). Early Christian apocryphal acts place a high value on continence. In many of their narratives, the decision to be continent coincides with conversion to Christian faith. Most of these acts date from the second half of the second century: for example, the Acts of Thomas from Syria, and the Acts of John and the Acts of Paul and Thecla from Asia Minor.

There was, therefore, a recognizable early Christian tendency toward continence, one with which John was likely to be familiar. The logic of his evaluation of continence has clear affinities with the thought of the Essenes. It is therefore likely that John held up continence as an ideal—for those who would "follow the Lamb wherever he goes." This ideal was closely related to the willingness to die for the faith which John also advocated. These ideals arise naturally from the apocalyptic mentality, which views the present situation in extreme terms. Christians are involved in a universal conflict that will determine their ultimate destinies. Life as it has been known is passing away. The world is corrupt and must be destroyed. Continence and voluntary death are intelligible responses of the individual Christian in such a framework.

WEALTH

The theme of wealth and poverty occurs at certain climactic points in the book of Revelation. The first occasion is the last of the seven messages, a passage that contains the final words of the one like a son of man, as he commissions John in the opening vision of the work (1:9–3:22). This last message (3:14–22) is directed to the Christians in Laodicea. They are criticized for being lukewarm and Christ threatens to vomit them out of his mouth.

In terms of the situation presupposed, this last message is similar to the one addressed to Thyatira. Some Christians in Thyatira apparently compromised their faith in John's eyes by mixing socially with influential local non-Christians. Such mixing probably involved a certain religious syncretism, at least in externals. Such behavior was very likely related to a desire to improve their economic situation. This surmise fits with what is known about Thyatira as a trading center with many guilds. Those members of the Christian community in Thyatira who refused such compromise are praised for their patient endurance. "Endurance," as we have seen, refers to taking and holding a public stand that leads to disadvantage and even death.

The Laodicean Christians were rich and probably of secure or even high social standing in the city. Their Christian faith was likely to be frowned upon by their Gentile associates. Nevertheless, their secure economic base freed them from some pressure to conform to polytheistic religious customs. Without powerful pressure of that sort— in John's eyes—they had become complacent. The message is intended to shake them out of their complacency. The description of Christ at the beginning already begins the process. Christ is the "faithful and true witness." The implied question is what the Laodiceans are doing by way of witness.

In the body of the message, the comfortable situation of the Christians in Laodicea is identified as "wretched, pitiable, poor, blind, and naked." They are living on the surface, a superficial life, without a sense of the deep struggle that is going on. They are counseled "to buy" from Christ "gold refined by fire." In other words, they are called to bear witness to the truth, as Christ did, in the full knowledge that such testimony leads to suffering.

It is likely that the Laodiceans had already been aware of the arrests, trials, discrimination, and at least one execution experienced by Christians in other cities. The message addressed to them implies that they counted themselves fortunate, even blessed by God, to have avoided such problems. But they are told, "Those whom I love, I reprove and chasten." Their peaceful existence is not a sign, in John's eyes, of God's favor, but of their own lack of zeal. This lack of zeal requires a change of heart: "Be zealous and repent."

The Christ of the messages proclaims the Laodiceans' wealth to be truly poverty. The opposite is said about the Christians in Smyrna: "I know your . . . poverty, but you are rich" (2:9). It is striking that the economically rich have nothing to fear from the authorities, whereas the poor are threatened with persecution. The underlying reason seems to be that it was possible to get and to maintain wealth only by accommodation to the polytheistic culture. The Jewish community would be an exception to this rule, since their beliefs and practices were recognized, if at times grudgingly, as an acceptable alternative, and their rights were protected by the Romans. It may be that the Laodicean Christians were Jewish or at least were on good terms with the local Jewish community. In any case, the advice of the Christ of the messages raises the question whether one could be both a faithful Christian and prosperous. John did not advocate turning oneself in to the authorities or giving away one's goods. Nevertheless, if the Laodiceans became zealous and repented, the result probably would not have been very different. The practice of zeal as John understood it very likely would have attracted the unfavorable attention of the authorities.

The theme of wealth appears again in chs. 17–18, passages discussed above under the rubric of attitude to the persecutors. Here it is enough to note that Rome is described as a harlot "arrayed in purple and scarlet, and bedecked with gold and jewels and pearls, holding in her hand a golden cup" (17:4). Purple and scarlet were colors of royalty. The gold, jewels, and pearls are obvious signs of wealth and luxury. In ch. 18 the theme of wealth and luxury dominates. A lengthy list of goods is given in connection with the wholesale dealers' mourning (18:12–13). Most of the goods mentioned are luxury items and would have been bought and sold only by the rich.

The final key passage in which the theme of wealth appears is in the "Jerusalem appendix," a section that is parallel to the "Babylon appendix," which was just discussed (17:1–19:10). The "Jerusalem appendix," 21:9–22:5, elaborates the vision of salvation that concludes the last series of visions in the book. When one ponders the social situation of the author of Revelation, the shape of the vision of Paradise described here is not surprising. Though he was often a visitor and perhaps occasionally a resident of many grand cities of Asia

Minor, John was probably not a citizen of any and was very likely regarded as an outsider by most citizens and many residents. He was probably dependent on the benevolence of others for his livelihood. This state of life, if not freely chosen, was at least consciously affirmed and accepted. But its hardships were amply compensated for in this hopeful vision of a city truly one's own, where the faithful would reign (22:5); a city to which the Gentiles would flock, and which exceeded even Ephesus, Smyrna, and Pergamum in the splendor of its public architecture. The impression of wealth and luxury is overwhelming. The city is like a jewel, like jasper or crystal (21:11). It is made of pure gold (21:18). The foundations of the wall of the city are adorned with twelve precious stones. These twelve stones were probably meant to call the cosmic symbolism of the Zodiac to mind, but that function is compatible with the sense of opulence they convey.[37] The twelve gates are each a single pearl, and the street is pure gold (21:21).

The presence of the theme of wealth at these climactic points in Revelation indicates, as we saw already in Chapter 3, that it was a problem for John. He criticized the Laodiceans' reliance on their wealth because it was evidence of their lack of zeal. Wealth was one of Rome's faults in John's eyes, presumably because Roman leaders and allies were felt to possess it at the expense of others. The vision of the new Jerusalem shows that John did not view wealth as evil in itself; rather, he saw it as one of the blessings of salvation to be granted in the future.

JOHN AS ITINERANT PROPHET

These strict teachings against social and economic accommodation and sexual relations go hand in hand with an intense apocalyptic mentality and an expectation of an imminent end of the world. Detachment from sexual, social, economic, and political life is feasible if one expects a sudden and speedy end to the world as we know it. But how could John have put such radical ideas into practice, and how could he have expected other early Christians to do so and to survive, even for a short time? John's radical teaching on social matters and his intense expectation of the end become imaginable and understandable if we conclude, for this and other reasons, that he was an itinerant prophet, one whose wandering embodied ascetic values with regard to home, family, wealth, civic politics—in sum, nearly all the ties of ordinary life.[38]

Wandering, that is, continual movement from place to place, was typical of Jesus, his disciples, and many leaders in the earliest church as these are portrayed in the Synoptic Gospels, Acts, and the letters of Paul. The motivation and rationale for such movement apparently varied. The basis for one type of itinerant life-style was evidently the imitation of Jesus. Such an imitation is reflected in certain sayings of the Synoptic tradition such as "Foxes have holes, and birds of the air have nests; but the Son of man has nowhere to lay his head" (Matt. 8:20 = Luke 9:58), and "Truly, I say to you, there is no one who has left house or wife or brothers or parents or children for the sake of the kingdom of God, who will not receive manifold more in this time, and in the age to come eternal life (Luke 18:29–30; see also Matt. 19:29; Mark 10:29–30). These two sayings illustrate asceticism with regard to home, marriage, and family ties.

The sayings in the Synoptic tradition that criticize wealth could have been spoken with greatest credibility by those who had no possessions of their own. They could proclaim, "It is easier for a camel to go through the eye of a needle than for a rich man to enter the kingdom of God" (Mark 10:25 = Matt. 19:24 = Luke 18:25). They could, with singleness of mind and heart, urge people: "Do not lay up for yourselves treasures on earth, where moth and rust consume and where thieves break in and steal, but lay up for yourselves treasures in heaven. . . . For where your treasure is, there will your heart be also" (Matt. 6:19–21; see also Luke 12:33–34).

Some of the special material in the Gospel of Matthew suggests that wandering prophets were still known and active in the region of the author and the first readers, which was probably Syria. In the Sermon on the Mount, Jesus teaches: "Beware of the false prophets, who come to you in sheep's clothing but inwardly are ravenous wolves. You will know them by their fruits" (Matt. 7:15–16). Luke has some of the same images, but not the reference to false prophets. The warning about false prophets suggests that there are also true prophets. The portrayal of them as coming implies that they were itinerant.

Matthew 10 presents a discourse of Jesus given on the occasion of his sending the twelve disciples out to preach, heal, and exorcise. Some of the material in this discourse is found also in Mark and much of it in Luke. But there are a number of elements which indicate that the commission of Jesus in Matthew 10 reflects the actual practice of wandering prophets. Only Matthew contains Jesus' remark, "You received without paying, give without pay" (Matt. 10:8b). The same is true of a saying near the end of the speech, "He who receives a prophet because he is a prophet shall receive a prophet's reward" (10:41). Matthew transposes to the middle of this discourse a passage from the so-called Synoptic Apocalypse, that is, from Mark 13 (Matt. 10:17–25). It is likely that in both Gospels this passage speaks quite directly to the situation of the first readers. Its placement in Matthew 10 shows that the wandering life was a live option for the first readers, and that some actually were living it.

In this discourse Jesus charges: "Take no gold, nor silver, nor copper in your belts, no bag for your journey, nor two tunics, nor sandals, nor a staff; for the laborer deserves his food. And whatever town or village you enter, find out who is worthy in it, and stay with him until you depart. . . . When they persecute you in one town, flee to the next; for truly, I say to you, you will not have gone through all the towns of Israel, before the Son of man comes" (Matt. 10:9–11, 23).

Evidence for ascetic wandering is also found in the Didache, that is, the *Teaching of the Twelve Apostles*. It is generally recognized that the text in its present form is the product of several stages of literary development.[39] It probably took on its present shape toward the end of the first century in Syria. The readers are instructed, "Whosoever then comes and teaches you all these things aforesaid, receive him" (11:1). Further, they are told,

> Let every Apostle who comes to you be received as the Lord, but let him not stay more than one day, or if need be a second as well; but if he stay three days, he is a false prophet. And when an Apostle goes forth let him accept nothing but bread till he reach his night's lodging; but if he ask for money, he is a false prophet. . . . But not everyone who speaks in a spirit is a prophet, except he have the behavior of the Lord. From his behavior, then, the false prophet and the true prophet shall be known. And no prophet who orders a meal in a spirit shall eat of it; otherwise he is a false prophet. . . . But whosoever shall say in a spirit, "Give me money, or something else," you shall not listen to him; but if he tell you to give on behalf of others in want, let none judge him. (11:4–6, 8–9, 12)[40]

As we saw in Chapter 1, John was probably a native or former resident of Palestine. It is likely that there were itinerant teachers, apostles, and prophets in Palestine as well as in Syria toward the end of the first century. The hypothesis that John was an ascetic wandering prophet illuminates much of the book of Revelation. It is supported by a variety of considerations. John has rivals in winning the allegiance of the Christians in the seven towns. The major rivals seem to be wandering leaders with whom he is in competition. The Ephesians are praised for testing those who call themselves apostles and finding them false (2:2). Apostles, as we know them elsewhere in early

Christian literature, generally traveled from place to place. Opponents at Ephesus, Pergamum, and Thyatira are criticized, all of whom apparently held the same teachings. This opposing movement was not a purely local phenomenon, but evidently was spread by itinerant leaders. It is noteworthy that the so-called "Jezebel" is not portrayed as a settled resident of Thyatira. The Thyatirans are admonished for "allowing or permitting her," perhaps to stay in one of their homes and to prophesy and teach them (2:20).

If John was an itinerant prophet, that fact would explain why he was familiar with each of the seven communities, but did not associate himself in any special way with any. It would also help explain why he does not mention bishops, elders, or deacons in any of the communities. He probably knew of their existence, but ignored their roles of leadership, because his was a different kind of authority and because he was perhaps in competition with them in influencing the points of view of the other readers.[41] The hypothesis also helps explain how John could have advocated teachings with such extreme political and social ramifications. He could condemn the wealth of Rome and the provincial elite with great detachment, integrity, and credibility. He could likewise challenge the readers not to participate in guilds, other associations, and some kinds of trade. He could present continence as an ideal.

This hypothesis also illuminates the tension between John and the Laodiceans. John did not insist that all his readers adopt the life-style to which he had been called. He probably recognized the need for some followers of the Lamb to lead settled lives and to earn a living for themselves and for hospitality to wandering leaders. But he apparently felt that the Laodiceans had gone too far in compromising with the world and were too tied to their goods and social status. His admonition, "Would that you were cold or hot!" reveals the difficulty one who would be perfect has with the compromises of life in this world.

On one level, the social crisis and trauma expressed in the Apocalypse was dealt with by a call to social radicalism. The response to the perceived crisis elicited by the book involves the establishment of Christian independence and identity by withdrawing from Greco-Roman society into an exclusive group with rigorous rules and an intense expectation of imminent judgment against their enemies and of their own salvation. No accommodation to polytheistic culture was allowed. Christians could not join any of the widespread unofficial societies for mutual benefit. Certain coins had to be avoided; detachment from wealth and property was demanded. Continence was held up as an ideal. Most of all, thoroughgoing opposition to Roman government was expected, a very radical stance indeed. On another level, the social crisis and trauma was dealt with by the creation of a new linguistic world. It is to this second response that we will turn in the next chapter.

NOTES

1. Adela Yarbro Collins, *The Combat Myth in the Book of Revelation* (Scholars Press, 1976), pp. 32–44.

2. R. H. Charles, *A Critical and Exegetical Commentary on the Revelation of St. John*, ICC (Charles Scribner's Sons, 1920), Vol. 1, pp. 172–174. For another opinion see Eduard Lohse, *Martyrer und Gottesknecht* (Göttingen: Vandenhoeck & Ruprecht, 1955), pp. 196–197.

3. On the prayer for or expectation of vengeance for the blood of the righteous, see 2 Macc. 7:36; 8:3; Assumption of Moses 9:6–7; *1 Enoch* 47:2, 4. On the fixed number of souls, see 4 Ezra 4:35–37, 41–43; *2 Baruch* 23:5 (see also 30:2). Like Rev. 6:9–11, *1 Enoch* 47:1–4 combines the two ideas.

4. Yarbro Collins, *The Combat Myth in the Book of Revelation*, pp. 158–161.

5. Ibid., pp. 172–183.

6. Ibid., pp. 16–19.

7. Hans Dieter Betz, "On the Problem of the Religio-Historical Understanding of Apocalypticism," in *Apocalypticism, Journal for Theology and the Church* 6, ed. by Robert W. Funk (1969), pp. 134–156; Adela Yarbro Collins, "The History-of-Religions Approach to Apocalypticism and the 'Angel of the Waters' (Rev. 16:4–7)," *CBQ* 39 (1977), pp. 367–381.

8. Yarbro Collins, "The History-of-Religions Approach to Apocalypticism," pp. 376–377.

9. Adela Yarbro Collins, "Revelation 18: Taunt-Song or Dirge?" in J. Lambrecht (ed.), *L'Apocalypse johannique et l'apocalyptique dans le Nouveau Testament* (Gembloux: J. Duculot, 1980), p. 185.

10. Ibid.

11. Ibid., pp. 185–186.

12. Ibid., p. 186.

13. Ibid., p. 192.

14. Ibid., p. 193.

15. Gerhard von Rad, *Old Testament Theology* (Harper & Row, 1965), Vol. 2, pp. 142, 229n16.

16. Nahum 3:4; 2 Chron. 33:6; 2 Kings 9:22; Micah 5:12.

17. *2 Baruch* 12:3; *Sib. Or.* 5:173–178.

18. Polybius, 3.3.9; Cicero, *De Re Publica* 3.23; Virgil, *Ecologue* 4.17; Juvenal, *Sat.* 8.87–124; Horace, *Epode* 16.

19. Mikhail Rostovtzeff, *The Social and Economic History of the Roman Empire* (Oxford: Clarendon Press, 1926), pp. 142–161.

20. David Magie, *Roman Rule in Asia Minor* (Princeton University Press, 1950), Vol. 1, p. 600.

21. Adolf Deissmann, *Light from the Ancient East* (Harper & Row, 1927), p. 341 and Fig. 62.

22. Charles, *A Critical and Exegetical Commentary on the Revelation of St. John,* Vol. 1, p. 362; G. Henton Davies, "Phylacteries," *IDB* 3 (1962), pp. 808–809.

23. Wilhelm Bousset, *Der Antichrist* (Göttingen: Vandenhoeck & Ruprecht, 1895), pp. 132–133.

24. Charles, *A Critical and Exegetical Commentary on the Revelation of St. John,* Vol. 1, p. 363.

25. G. B. Caird, *A Commentary on the Revelation of St. John the Divine* (Harper & Row, 1966), p. 173.

26. Adela Yarbro Collins, "The Political Perspective of the Revelation to John," *JBL* 96 (1977), p. 253.

27. Ibid., pp. 253–254.

28. F. Blass and A. Debrunner, *A Greek Grammar of the New Testament and Other Early Christian Literature* (University of Chicago Press, 1961), pp. 152–153.

29. Philo, *Hypothetica* 14; cited by A. Dupont-Sommer, *The Essene Writings from Qumran* (Gloucester, Mass.: Peter Smith, 1973), p. 25.

30. Philo, *Hypothetica* 3; cited in Dupont-Sommer, p. 24.

31. Josephus, *Jewish War* 2.120–121, 160–161.

32. CD 7:6–7; translation by Géza Vermès, *The Dead Sea Scrolls in English* (Penguin Books, 1962), pp. 103–104.

33. 1QSa 1:4, 9–10.

34. Frank Moore Cross, Jr., *The Ancient Library of Qumran and Modern Biblical Studies* (Doubleday & Co., 1961), p. 97.

35. Ibid., pp. 98–99, 237–238.

36. Frank Moore Cross, Jr., *Canaanite Myth and Hebrew Epic* (Harvard University Press, 1973), pp. 105–106; Patrick D. Miller, Jr., *The Divine Warrior in Early Israel* (Harvard University Press, 1973), pp. 64–65; Yarbro Collins, *The Combat Myth in the Book of Revelation*, pp. 130–145, 157–190, 231–234.

37. R. H. Charles recognized an allusion to the symbolism of the Zodiac, but thought it was polemical (*A Critical and Exegetical Commentary on the Revelation of St. John*, Vol. 2, pp. 165–169). Recent research has supported his judgment that there is indeed an allusion to the Zodiac; the allusion was probably a positive one (Adela Yarbro Collins, "Numerical Symbolism in Jewish and Early Christian Apocalyptic Literature," *ANRW* II.21).

38. Gerd Theissen, *Sociology of Early Palestinian Christianity* (Fortress Press, 1978).

39. R. A. Kraft, "Apostolic Fathers 4," IDBSup (1976), pp. 36–37.

40. Translation by Kirsopp Lake, *The Apostolic Fathers* (LCL), Vol. 1.

41. David Aune, "The Social Matrix of the Apocalypse of John," *BR* 26 (1981), p. 27.

5

The Power of Apocalyptic Rhetoric–Catharsis

The purpose of this chapter is to show *what* the book of Revelation does and *how* it does it. In other words, this chapter focuses on the effect the Apocalypse had on its first readers and how it achieved that effect. The task of Revelation was to overcome the unbearable tension perceived by the author between what was and what ought to have been. His purpose was to create that tension for readers unaware of it, to heighten it for those who felt it already, and then to overcome it in an act of literary imagination. In the literary creation which is the Apocalypse, the tension between what was and what ought to be is manifest in the opposition between symbols of God's rule and symbols of Satan's rule, between symbols of the authority and power of Christ and symbols of the authority and power of Caesar.

When one reflects upon the symbols of the Apocalypse in the light of its historical situation, one sees that its task is to overcome the intolerable tension between reality and hopeful faith. Sociologists speak of such tension as cognitive dissonance, a state of mind that arises when there is great disparity between expectations and reality.[1] Tension between what is and what ought to be is reflected in Revelation in the sharp contradiction set up between symbols and sets of symbols. All living beings are given a place in a dualistic structure. At the pinnacle of power on one side is God, the Pantocrator, ruler of all (1:8). On the other is Satan, the Dragon, who has power, a throne, and great authority (13:2). Allied with God is the Lamb who was slain (5:6); this is the one like a son of man who died and is alive for evermore (1:18). Allied with Satan is the beast from the sea (13:1–2), which was wounded with a mortal wound and yet lived (13:3, 14). All the people of the earth are divided into two groups; those who have the seal of God on their foreheads and whose names are in the

book of life (3:5, 12; 7:3; 20:4; 21:27; 22:4) and those who bear the
mark of the beast and worship it (9:4; 13:8, 17; 14:9–11; 16:2; 20:15).
There is also a sharp contrast drawn between the luxurious and
voluptuous harlot, who represents Babylon, the earthly city of abominations (ch. 17) and the pure bride of the Lamb, who symbolizes
Jerusalem, the heavenly city of salvation (19:7–8; 21:2, 9–11).

This literary tension reflects the political tension between the ad-
herents of the kingdom of God and those of the kingdom of Caesar
(11:15; 12:10; 16:10; 17:18). Both claim dominion over the whole
earth and eternal rule. The sharp contradictions set up between symbols and sets of symbols suggest that the Apocalypse is mythic narrative as it is defined by the French anthropologist Claude Lévi-Strauss.
He has argued that "the purpose of myth is to provide a logical model
capable of overcoming a contradiction."[2] Myths mediate unwelcome
contradictions, that is, they make them appear less final and thus
more acceptable.[3] If the contradiction is real, mediation thus produces
a theoretically infinite number of attempts at overcoming the contradiction, each different in detail, but the same in underlying structure.[4]
The impossibility, at least in John's circumstances and from his point
of view, of mediating the contradiction between the rule of God and
the rule of Caesar would help explain why we have so much repetition
in the Apocalypse. Beginning with the seven seals, each series of seven
is an attempt to overcome this contradiction. Each series is distinctive
in its particular formulations of character and plot. Beneath this
variety of surface texture, however, is the same formal structure. In
each series the contradiction between followers of the Lamb and
followers of the beast is presented and overcome by the triumph of
the Lamb.

WHAT OUGHT TO BE

A vision of what ought to be is expressed in the symbols related
to God and Christ in the Apocalypse. In ch. 4 God is portrayed as
king and creator. God is the enthroned one surrounded by various
officers of the heavenly court. The hymn of the elders acclaims God
worthy of glory, honor, and power, because the enthroned one has
created all things. Near the beginning of the book, God is given the
title Pantocrator, ruler of all (1:8). It is a common title of God in
Revelation, occurring in eight other passages. One of the climaxes of
the book is the announcement that "the kingdom of the world has
become the kingdom of our Lord and of his Christ, and he shall reign
for ever and ever" (11:15).

In 1:5 Jesus is called the ruler of the kings of the earth. In the message to Pergamum, the sharp two-edged sword of the one like a son of man is implicitly contrasted with the "sword" of the Roman governor which slew Antipas (2:12–13). The son of God is portrayed as the one who has power over the nations (2:18, 26–27). The exalted Christ is enthroned with God (3:21). He is given the traditional national messianic titles "Lion of the tribe of Judah" and "the Root of David" (5:5). He is given the titles "King of kings" and "Lord of lords," which have obvious political connotations (19:16). He is portrayed as king in the messianic reign of a thousand years (20:4–6).

These symbols and their use in Revelation suggest that some early Christians expected the rule of God announced by Jesus to be a public affair. They expected God's rule to involve the whole person, the outer as well as the inner self. They expected the social, economic, and political order to be changed, speedily and thoroughly, not just that another voluntary association would take its place beside the others. This public transformation of reality was expected to involve at least autonomy for the faithful, if not power over others. All the faithful have been made priests (1:6; 5:10). The one who conquers will rule over the nations with a rod of iron (2:27). All the faithful will reign on earth (5:10; see also 22:5).

The early Christian perspective reflected in the Apocalypse shares with the Zealots and related Jewish groups the conviction that God's rule must be manifest in concrete political ways and that acknowledgment of God's rule is incompatible with submission to Rome. "Behold, he is coming with the clouds, and every eye will see him, every one who pierced him; and all the tribes of the earth will wail on account of him. Even so. Amen" (1:7). The starting point of Revelation is that Jesus and his followers must have public and communal vindication, in the here and now and soon. The transformation of individuals, inner freedom, a personal afterlife—these elements alone were an insufficient, incomplete manifestation of salvation.

Such were the hopes, the expectations of what ought to be. In striking contrast to the hope was the reality. By the light of the historical context, we may read in the pages of Revelation evidence of a perceived social crisis and personal and communal trauma, as we saw in Chapter 3. The perceived social crisis and traumatic experiences apparently led to certain feelings that are reflected and dealt with in the Apocalypse. A feeling of powerlessness was evoked by the exclusion of Christians from Jewish and Gentile institutions. Fear was elicited by the denunciation of Christians before Roman authorities and by the impressions left by the traumas of Nero's persecution, the destruction of Jerusalem, the execution of Antipas, and John's banishment. Aggressive feelings were aroused by the various social tensions. Resentment was felt at the rejection and hostility of Jews and Gentiles. Envy of the autonomous, the wealthy, and the powerful rankled. The imperial ruler cult evoked antipathy and frustration. The violent deeds of the Roman Empire called forth a desire for vengeance.

HOW THE APOCALYPSE CREATES ITS EFFECT

In reflecting upon how the Apocalypse does what it does, the first thing to consider is the type of language to which it belongs. Words are used in a wide variety of ways, among which are: (1) to talk about people, things, and ideas (informative language); (2) to think (cognitive language); (3) to display attitudes and feelings (expressive language); and (4) to elicit attitudes and feelings (evocative language). Informative and cognitive language may be called referential, in that the words refer to generally recognizable entities.[5]

To some extent the language of the book of Revelation is referential. It is that quality which allows us to relate the book to its historical context and to discover social information in its pages. But the primary purpose of the book is not to impart information. It is rather to call for *commitment* to the actions, attitudes, and feelings uttered. It is thus primarily commissive language.[6] In particular, it is expressive and evocative language. It makes no attempt to report events or to describe people in a way that everyone could accept. Rather, it provides a highly selective and perspectival view. Like a poem, it presents and interprets some aspect of reality, expresses a response to it, and invites the reader or hearer to share in the interpretation and the response.

As expressive language, the book of Revelation creates a virtual experience for the hearer or reader. It is likely that the Apocalypse was read aloud before the assembled Christians of a given locality, perhaps at regular intervals. A beatitude is pronounced near the beginning, "Blessed is he who reads aloud the words of the prophecy, and blessed are those who hear, and who keep what is written therein; for the time is near" (1:3). For this reason it is better to speak of the first "hearers" of Revelation, rather than the "readers."

The Apocalypse is as evocative as it is expressive. Not only does it display attitudes and feelings; it also elicits them. One can go even further and say that the Apocalypse creates its effect by manipulating the thoughts, attitudes, and feelings of the hearers. I am using the word "manipulate" here in the neutral sense of handling with skill or art. I do not intend the negative sense of unfairness, fraud, or falsification due to self-interest. The Apocalypse handles skillfully the hearers' thoughts, attitudes, and feelings by the use of effective symbols and a narrative plot that invites imaginative participation. This combination of effective symbols and artful plot is the key to the power of apocalyptic rhetoric.

NARRATIVE TECHNIQUES
AND THEIR EMOTIONAL EFFECT

Various techniques may be observed in the use of effective symbols and the construction of plot. The most fundamental technique and the one that underlies and reinforces all the others is the presentation of the Apocalypse as an authoritative, true, and trustworthy revelation of heavenly origin. It is claimed that the revelation comes from the highest authority, from God, who gave it to Jesus Christ, who entrusted it to an angel, who communicated it to John (1:1). The hearer is assured of the truthfulness of John's testimony (1:2). This characterization of the content of the book is reinforced by the use of vision accounts and the reports of auditions. The hearer is given the impression that John is handing on the revelation just as he received it. The claims and assurances about the origin and reliability of the revelation are repeated several times near the end of the book (22:6–10, 16; see also 18–20). It is likely that the effectiveness of the Apocalypse for the first hearers depended upon belief in these claims. Such belief is very important today for fundamentalist readers of Revelation. Critical readers, however, take the position that the validity of the book must be determined through an assessment of its content, quite apart from the question of its origin.

A second technique is the reinterpretation of prophecy and of other texts in the Jewish Bible read as prophecy. The effectiveness of this technique depended on the continuing belief in the authority and reliability of the prophets of the Jewish Bible and on the assumption that they prophesied, not about their own times, but about the end of days. Like the Essenes at Qumran, the early Christians believed that they were living during the last days. As the Essenes believed that their Teacher of Righteousness had received the interpretative key by divine revelation to the mysteries of the biblical texts, so the early Christians believed that their prophets, apostles, and teachers could expound the true meaning of such texts, because they were enlightened by the teaching of Jesus Christ and the Holy Spirit.

This technique is evident in a saying quoted earlier, "Behold, he is coming with the clouds, and every eye will see him, every one who pierced him; and all the tribes of the earth will wail on account of him" (1:7). The mysterious description of one like a son of man in Dan. 7:13 and the obscure prediction of Zech. 12:10–14 are regarded as unfulfilled prophecies. The two are combined and reinterpreted as a prediction of the second coming of Christ as judge in the Final Judgment. The underlying conviction is that Daniel and Zechariah predicted events in the near future of the hearers of Revelation.

Just as the book of Daniel updated and reinterpreted Jeremiah's prophecy that the desolations of Jerusalem would last seventy years, so the book of Revelation reinterprets and applies to its own situation the prophecy in Daniel that the shattering of the power of the holy people would last for a time, two times, and half a time (Dan. 7:25; 12:7). Each "time" in Daniel represents about a year (see Dan. 8: 13–14; 9:27; 12:11–12). The vision of the angel who announces the nearness of the end in Revelation 10 is heavily reminiscent of the angel in Daniel 12 who says that salvation will come after three and a half "times." The Gentiles, it is predicted, will trample the holy city for forty-two months (three and one half years; Rev. 11:2). The two witnesses will prophesy for one thousand two hundred and sixty days (three and one half years; 11:3). The woman clothed with the sun, it is said, will be nourished in the desert for a time, and times, and a half a time (12:14). Earlier her sojourn is described as lasting one thousand two hundred and sixty days (three and a half years, 12:6). Finally, the beast from the sea will exercise authority for forty-two months (three and a half years; 13:5). It is quite easy to conclude that the author of Daniel actually made calculations and to associate the three and one half years with the period between the defilement of the temple and its rededication. It is virtually impossible to do anything of the sort with Revelation. It is likely that John adopted the designation of a period of final crisis from Daniel and believed that the prophecy of Daniel 12 would be fulfilled in his own time. It is unlikely that he made any precise calculations.

When Daniel 7 was composed, the fourth and most terrifying beast represented the Greco-Syrian kingdom with which its first readers had to contend. In ch. 13, the fourth beast of Daniel (or perhaps all four beasts combined) is interpreted as a prophecy of the Roman Empire. If John knew of the application of Daniel 7 to the situation under Antiochus Epiphanes, he would have considered it incorrect or merely preliminary. Daniel was viewed as a prophecy referring to John's and his hearers' own time.

Another literary technique is the use of traditional symbols in the composition of allegorical narrative. A borderline case between this technique and the previous one is the use of the names Balaam and Jezebel in the messages to Pergamum and Thyatira. From one point of view, the hearers could infer that the narratives in Numbers and 1 and 2 Kings were written for the instruction of the believers of the last days and that the characters Balaam and Jezebel in those narratives were really false teachers contemporary with themselves. From another point of view, these names were already traditional symbols. The hearers were being invited to see analogies between classic situations in Israel's past and their own situations. They were being called upon to think typologically. Typology is a way of thinking that is similar to allegory. An archetype is used to give meaning to a present event. The effectiveness of this technique, if it be accepted, is obvious and powerful. The nameless man who had a following at Pergamum is no longer a fellow Christian who holds opinions and teaches practices that must be evaluated on their merits. Suddenly he is Balaam, who led Israel into idolatry and harlotry; these deeds angered the Lord and provoked him to send a plague upon Israel (Num. 25:1–9; 31:16). The implication for the hearers is plain: if they listen to this man's teaching they will be punished by God. The same dynamic is present in giving the name "Jezebel" to the prophet who had a following in Thyatira.

The allegorical technique is also evident in the visions of the seven trumpets and the seven bowls. Both the image of the trumpet and that of the bowl have their own connotations, which contribute to the effect of the narrative. The focus here is on the similarity these visions have with the narratives about the plagues against Egypt which the Lord sent through Moses, according to Exodus 7–12. Among the allusions are water turning to blood (Rev. 8:9; 16:4; Ex. 7:14–24) and a plague of locusts (Rev. 9:1–11; Ex. 10:1–20). The plagues of the trumpets and bowls are presented in Revelation as punishment upon the earth, especially upon the Romans, for the unjust shedding of blood, especially for the murder of faithful Christians. The use of the traditional symbol of the plague suggested to the hearers that they understand their own situation by analogy with the slavery of the Israelites in Egypt. The cognitive dissonance or tension between their expectations and their experience was reduced by suggesting that their own hardships would be resolved as those of the Israelite slaves were. As God delivered Israel from Egypt, so he would deliver Christians from Rome.

Perhaps the most powerful use of this technique is the presentation of the hearers' opponents as symbols of chaos and the resolution of the conflict between the hearers and their opponents through narratives whose plots conform to the traditional myths of combat and creation. Chapter 13 contains a vision of a beast rising out of the sea. Several elements suggest that this beast symbolizes the Roman Empire. It has dominion over the whole earth (v. 7b), it is worshiped by many people (vs. 4, 8), and it attacks the saints (v. 7a). The portrait of the beast from the sea draws upon a number of closely related traditional symbols. It contains allusions to features of Daniel 7 and 8. As we have seen, Daniel's vision of four kingdoms is presented indirectly as a prophecy fulfilled in Revelation's own time. But the images of Daniel were already traditional. The beasts rising from the sea called to mind Yahweh's battles with Leviathan and Rahab, those sea monsters whose rebellion against God symbolized the forces of chaos, sterility, and death. Their defeat represents the victory of order, fertility, and life, which is associated with God's creative acts. These symbols were not unique to Israel. They were common in narratives of combat and creation in various cultures of the ancient and the Hellenistic Near East. There are clear indications in Revelation that such symbols are not archaic survivals, but living symbols arising out of a mythopoetic consciousness.[7]

The plots of ancient myths of combat vary, but they have certain elements in common. A rebellion, usually led by a dragon or other beast, threatens the reigning gods, or the king of the gods. Sometimes the ruling god is defeated, even killed, and then the dragon reigns in chaos for a time. Finally the beast is defeated by the god who ruled before, or some ally of his. Following his victory the reestablished king of the gods (or a new, young king in his stead) builds his house or temple, marries and produces offspring, or hosts a great banquet. These latter elements represent the reestablishment of order and fertility.

This basic plot or pattern is found in every series of visions in Revelation, beginning with the seven seals. It is found in brief form, for example, in ch. 12, and in more elaborate form, for example, in the passage that extends from 19:11 to 22:5. In ch. 12, the dragon rebels against God by attempting to destroy the agent of God who is about to be born. This hostile act implies that the dragon is attempting to become king himself. His association with chaos is clear from his sweeping down stars from the sky with his tail (v. 4). The battle comes in vs. 7–9. Michael, ally of God and the child, defeats the dragon and casts him out of heaven. The result is the reestablishment of God's kingship in heaven (v. 10). But a further consequence of the casting down of the dragon is a dragon's reign on earth (v. 12b–17). This reign is characterized by chaos, as the spewing out of water from the dragon's mouth shows.

In this chapter, vs. 1–9 and 13–17 are narrative. Verses 10–12 comprise a hymn that provides a kind of commentary on the narrative. The dragon's attack on the woman and the child is interpreted as Satan's attempt to malign Christians in the heavenly court in his role as accuser. The throwing of the dragon down out of heaven is presented as equivalent to the victory of Christians over Satan by means of Christ's death, their own testimony, and their willingness to die. The image of the heavenly court calls earthly courts to mind. Although Christians who hold on to their faith are found guilty in the earthly courts, they are acquitted in the heavenly court, whose judgment alone truly matters. Thus, the hymn suggests that the narrative of ch. 12 is allegorical, not in the sense that each character or event in the story can be identified with some character or event in ordinary time, space, and history. Rather, it is allegorical in the sense that the whole narrative expresses in symbolic form the predicament of the hearers and provides it with a resolution. The hearers are invited to identify with the woman. Like Israel at the time of the exodus she is carried to safety by eagles' wings. Like Israel she is nourished in the desert by God. The traditional narrative of the exodus reinforces the narrative of ch. 12 in assuring the hearers that they will not be overwhelmed by the threat that Rome poses to them.

The passage that extends from 19:11 to 22:5 is the climax of the Apocalypse. As we have seen, the book of Revelation consists of six sections apart from prologue and epilogue: (1) the seven messages, (2) the seven seals, (3) the seven trumpets, (4) seven unnumbered visions, (5) the seven bowls plus a Babylon appendix, (6) seven unnumbered visions plus a Jerusalem appendix.[8] The seven messages constitute a distinct section in which the hearers are directly admonished and encouraged. The other five sections recapitulate each other; that is, they all have the same basic plot. As we have seen, each section implies a movement from persecution of the faithful, to punishment of the opponents of the faithful, to salvation of the faithful. This narrative movement which is repeated conforms to the basic plot shared by the ancient myths of combat: threat of rebellion, combat-victory (defeat of rebels), and kingship (salvation, order, fertility).[9]

The last section of the Apocalypse begins with a theophany of the divine warrior (19:11–16). The threat or rebellion is presupposed. Verse 11 picks up a thread of narrative dropped at 16:16 where the dragon and the two beasts of ch. 13 are gathering the kings of the earth for the final battle. In 19:17–18 the victory banquet is depicted as a feast of birds upon the flesh of the fallen. In Isa. 34:7 the bodies of the slain are portrayed as a sacrifice that makes the land fertile. The banquet motif in Revelation 19 reflects an ancient form of the idea that the hero's victory leads to renewed fertility. In the messianic reign (20:4–6) the kingdom of the newly established king, Christ, is manifested. The fertility of the restored order is expressed in the creation of a new heaven and earth (21:1) and in the manifestation of the water of life and the tree of life (22:1–2). Fertility and order are also expressed, at least in a sublimated way, in the sacred marriage of the Lamb (21:2, 9). The presentation of the new Jerusalem takes the place of temple-building or palace-building in other narratives.

The presentation of the hearers' struggle with Rome as a new form of the old conflict between order and chaos clarified their situation for the hearers and gave it meaning. The movement of the plot then instilled the conviction that the heavens ultimately would be victorious, as the forces of order always triumph in the myth. To be effective this narrative resolution of the crisis must be believable. The first hearers were likely to have found it so, since they were attuned to the perspective of myth, and since every people of the Greco-Roman world had at least one version of the combat or creation myth. The archaic and universal nature of the mythic pattern reflected in Revelation lends a certain authority and credence to its underlying message. As it was in the beginning, as it always has been when the chaos monster rears its head, so it will be once again. God and the Lamb, as representatives of creation, life, and order, will be victorious over the dragon and his two bestial allies.

It is likely that Rev. 11:3–13, the narrative about the two witnesses, has a function similar to that of the narrative about the woman and the dragon in ch. 12. The witnesses are identified as "the two olive trees and the two lampstands which stand before the Lord of the earth" (11:4). This identification calls to mind one of the visions of Zechariah. The prophet sees "two branches of the olive trees" and "two golden pipes from which the oil is poured out" (Zech. 4:12). An angel tells him that these represent "the two anointed who stand by the Lord of the whole earth" (Zech. 4:14). Once again, John is using an old story, traditional images, to interpret his own situation. In the context of Zechariah, the two anointed ones are the new Davidic ruler (Zerubbabel) and the new high priest (Joshua).

If John adverted to that interpretation at all, he would have seen Zerubbabel and Joshua as, at most, prototypes of the two witnesses of the end time. There is nothing in the Apocalypse that implies the coming of a Davidic and a priestly messiah. John's assumption probably was that the passage in Zechariah was about to be fulfilled in a way the Jewish prophet did not foresee. The activity of each of the witnesses recalls the mighty deeds of Moses and Elijah, as well as the ministry and destiny of Jesus. If "any one would harm them," they have power to destroy "their foes by fire." This element recalls one of the stories about Elijah (2 Kings 1:9–12; Sir. 48:3). Their "power to shut the sky, that no rain may fall during the days of their prophesying" recalls an even more famous story about Elijah (1 Kings 17–18; Sir. 48:3; Luke 4:25; James 5:17). The "power over the waters to turn them into blood, and to smite the earth with every plague" recalls the role of Moses as God's agent in smiting the Egyptians, especially his turning the Nile and all the waters of Egypt into blood (Ex. 7:14–19).

The two witnesses will be killed in Jerusalem, where "their Lord was crucified." Their bodies will lie unburied for "three days and a half"; then God will bring them back to life (v. 11). Finally, they will go up to heaven in a cloud (v. 12). The basic pattern of the witnesses' destiny very clearly repeats that of Jesus' ministry: a prophetic ministry including mighty deeds, violent death in Jerusalem, resurrection and ascension. The ascension of the two witnesses also reminds the hearers of Elijah's ascension in a chariot (2 Kings 2:11). Moses was also thought to have ascended to heaven. Such a tradition is probably reflected in Jude 9.

Many theories have been proposed on the identity of the two witnesses and the time of their appearance. One theory is that they are historical figures, Peter and Paul. Another theory holds that the vision is, from John's point of view, an as yet unfulfilled prophecy of the return of Moses and Elijah or of two superhuman forerunners of the second coming of Christ. It is difficult, if not impossible, to determine how John himself understood this vision. It is perhaps significant that he did not name the two witnesses. The anonymity of the witnesses suggests that the importance of the story was not so much its who or when, but the fact that it provides a point of orientation for the hearers. Like the two characters in the story, the hearers aspired to being God's witnesses, to giving testimony about God's cause in the world. At least it is clear that John wished them so to aspire. They too are confident of God's protection, even though they may be called upon to endure hardships, suffering, even violent death. God's protection is expected in their everyday lives and beyond and in spite of death. This protection is described in spectacular ways in the story. It may well be that John and the hearers of the book experienced and expected spectacular assistance. The ministry of Jesus, and that of at least some apostles and prophets, seems to have been accompanied by extraordinary phenomena such as healing and exorcism. The allusions to the signs of Elijah and Moses may be hyperbolic reflections of such phenomena, actual and expected. The hope of resurrection was probably held quite literally. It is striking that the witnesses are raised and ascend in the sight of their foes (v. 11–12). That element reflects the desire for public vindication evident also in 1:7 and 3:9. In any case, the spectacular divine intervention expresses in a symbolic way the deep trust that God's cause, as John sees it, is just, true, and worth dying for. The intervention of God does not eliminate the necessity of dying.

Death in this narrative is at the hands of "the beast which ascends from the bottomless pit." The pit represents the underworld where the forces of chaos are often confined in the combat and creation myths. The ascension of the beast from the pit implies that the forces which oppose the testimony of God's witnesses are part of the constant struggle of death with life, of destruction with creation, of order with chaos.

The techniques just described are ways in which the thoughts, attitudes, and feelings of the hearers were skillfully handled. The feeling of powerlessness due to the marginal social situation of the hearers was mitigated by the assurance that they had access to privileged information, to revealed truth of heavenly origin. At a deeper level, the hearers' powerlessness and lack of control over events is not denied, but affirmed. It is of little importance, however, because they are God's and God is in control. The reinterpretation of prophecy and the use of typology and allegory imply that the course of events has been fixed. The forces of chaos are dominant now, but their defeat is certain.

Likewise, the fear of the hearers is not denied or minimized. On the contrary, it is intensified. The hostile Jews and Roman authorities are not just ill-disposed human beings, but they have all the power of Satan on their side. Just as death, disease, and the failure of crops are ever-recurring evils, so these hostile political forces will not be overcome easily. The symbols and plot promise victory and new life, but it is on the other side of suffering and death.

THE PROCESS OF CATHARSIS

There is a certain analogy between Aristotle's explanation of the function of Greek tragedy and the function of Revelation. In each case certain emotions are aroused and then a catharsis of those emotions is achieved. Tragedy manipulates the emotions of fear and pity; Revelation, primarily fear and resentment. Aristotle's term "catharsis" is a medical metaphor. In its medical sense it refers to the removal from the body of alien matter that is painful and the restoration of the system to its normal state. The relation between this medical sense and Aristotle's application of the term to tragedy has been much debated.[10] He does not appear to have meant that the emotions of fear and pity are removed by tragedy, but only that their painful or disquieting elements are removed. Fear and pity in daily life can be disquieting for at least two reasons. Such feelings are often inarticulate, vague, and thus difficult to deal with. Also, they relate to people and events that are very close to home and thus especially threatening. This threatening character applies also to pity in Aristotle's understanding: we pity others where under like circumstances we would fear for ourselves. The emotions of the audience are purged in the sense that their feelings of fear and pity are intensified and given objective expression. The feelings are thus brought to consciousness and become less threatening.

Revelation functions in a similar way. Fear of Roman power is evoked or intensified. In various symbolic narratives, conflicts are described, each of which is a paradigm of the hearers' situation. As we have seen, the hearers' destiny is symbolized by the story of the two witnesses in ch. 11 and of the woman in ch. 12. The powers that threaten them are symbolized by the beast from the abyss and the dragon. These vivid images are certainly designed more to evoke terror than to allay it. Nevertheless, the projection of the conflict onto a cosmic screen, as it were, is cathartic in the sense that it clarifies and objectifies the conflict. Fearful feelings are vented by the very act of expressing them, especially in this larger-than-life and exaggerated way.

Resentment of Roman wealth and power is evoked or intensified especially in chs. 17 and 18. The great harlot Babylon is arrayed in purple and scarlet, adorned with gold, jewels, and pearls; she drinks from a golden cup (17:4; 18:16). The merchants are portrayed mourning over their cargo of luxury goods: "gold, silver, jewels and pearls, fine linen, purple, silk, and scarlet, all kinds of scented wood, all articles of ivory, all articles of costly wood, bronze, iron and marble, cinnamon, spice, incense, myrrh, frankincense, wine, oil, fine flour and wheat, cattle and sheep, horses and chariots, and slaves, that is, human souls" (18:12–13). This list is purposely selective and perspectival. The major cargo carried on Roman seas was grain. It was from the transportation of grain that the fortunes under the Flavians were made. This list emphasizes the luxury items, goods which the hearers either had no hope of attaining or were expected to forego. All these alluring, unattainable goods are to be destroyed by divine wrath.

Revelation produces a catharsis not only by means of individual symbolic narratives but by the structure of the book as a whole. Feelings of fear and resentment are released by the book's repeated presentations of the destruction of the hearers' enemies. The element of persecution represents the present, conflict-ridden, and threatened situation in which the author invites the hearers to see themselves. The second two elements in the repeated plot, judgment and salvation, represent the resolution of that situation: the persecutors are destroyed by divine wrath and the persecuted are exalted to a new, glorious mode of existence.

PSYCHOLOGICAL DYNAMICS

The effect of the symbols and plot of the Apocalypse was to reduce cognitive dissonance in two related ways. First, disquieting, disruptive feelings were released in a literary, experiential process of catharsis. Second, the conviction was instilled in the hearers that what ought to be *is*. The content of Revelation involves a hidden heavenly reality that shows the visible world to be radically different from what it seems. Jesus, though slain, is exalted in heaven and controls the destiny of the world (ch. 5). Although his followers are powerless, he is the true king, the ruler of the kings of the earth. In spite of the divine honors accorded to Rome and its agents, Satan is the real source of its power, not heaven (chs. 12 and 13). What ought to be *is* also in the already determined future. The content of the book also involves a future reality in which the earthly realm will be fully and manifestly determined by the heavenly world, that is, by God and Christ. Although this process was probably not conscious, what ought to be was experienced as a present reality by the hearers in the linguistic and imaginative event of hearing the book read. If the book was read in the context of worship, this effect would have been even stronger. As a gathered community before God, the hearers would have experienced in the imagination the heavenly reality and the determined future in which John was calling them to believe.

From a social-psychological viewpoint, the vision of a heavenly reality and of a radically new future functions as compensation for the relatively disadvantaged situation of the hearers or as an imaginative way of resolving the tension between expectations and social reality. There is a certain analogy between the creative imagination of the schizophrenic and the vision of the Apocalypse. According to Harold

Searles, the tragedy of a schizophrenic's life is very much of a piece with the tragedy of life for all human beings.[11] Ernest Becker agreed and defined that tragedy as the fact of human finitude, one's dread of death, and the overwhelmingness of life.[12] All human beings are faced with an existential dilemma. This dilemma is rooted, in Erich Fromm's words, in the fact that humankind is half animal and half symbolic.[13] Our animal nature presents us with the necessity of living within certain limits. Our symbolic nature allows us to challenge those limits, to transcend them at least in the imagination, by the pursuit of possibility.

The schizophrenic feels the pain of the human existential dilemma more acutely than others because he or she does not have "the confident defenses that a person normally uses to deny" it.[14] By means of elaborate fantasies, the schizophrenic is able to live with the terror of reality. In this mental state, a person overvalues the powers of the symbolic self and one loses oneself in the pursuit of possibility.[15] Such a way of life is marvelously creative, but ultimately maladaptive and dysfunctional.

The book of Revelation takes messianic language about Jesus very seriously and refuses to eliminate or minimize the social and political dimensions of messianic hope. As we have seen, such a preunderstanding made it very difficult if not impossible to make sense of the current sociopolitical situation of Christians. The solution of the Apocalypse is an act of creative imagination which, like that of the schizophrenic, withdraws from empirical reality, from real experience in the everyday world. According to the anthropologist George De Vos, an individual can deal with inner tensions by devising a projective system. It takes a great deal of energy to maintain such a system, however; if the burden of maintenance becomes unbearable, such an individual may lapse into pathological behavior. Inner stresses are more effectively controlled by collectively held and socially reinforced beliefs, since it takes less energy to believe in a social myth than to create and maintain one's own. De Vos goes on to say that

> social projections shared collectively within a group permit some form of psychic balance to be maintained without any overt social malfunctioning. Under ordinary conditions overt conflict does not appear. However, when stress becomes unmanageable, some overt form of violence may erupt.[16]

These considerations call to mind two frequent criticisms of the Apocalypse. It is often said of the book of Revelation and other apocalyptic texts that they are pessimistic, passive, a lapse from human activity into mythology. Similarly, millenarian movements have been called "prepolitical." These assessments are quite accurate to a point. It is God or some other superhuman figure who will act to bring in the millennium. Humanity is to endure and wait. As we have seen, John urged his readers indirectly to avoid participation in civic and political life. Nevertheless, the symbols and plot of Revelation, when deeply heard, do affect the actions of the hearers. It is a text that enables hearers or readers to cope in extreme circumstances. In a situation where direct political action is not feasible, it is a text that keeps alive the expectation of a better world.

Another criticism of the Apocalypse focuses on its violent language. It by no means advocates violence of humans against others. Nevertheless, violent imagery is prominent. The attitude toward violence in the book thus seems ambivalent. It can be explored in relation to the concept of aggression.

The Apocalypse may be viewed fruitfully as part of a process of containing aggressive feelings.[17] As we have seen, it is likely that the social tensions evident in the historical setting of Revelation gave rise to aggressive feelings on the part of the author and some of the hearers. There was probably resentment at the rejection and hostility of many Jews and Gentiles, envy and resentment of the autonomous, wealthy, and powerful, a desire for vengeance against Rome, and competitive and even hostile feelings toward other Christians with whom one disagreed. The book of Revelation provides evidence for a dynamic process involving two methods of containing such aggressive feelings.

The first of these is the transference of aggression felt by the author or the hearers to another subject. When aggressive action is not desirable and aggressive feelings cannot simply be suppressed or converted into other feelings and activities, the aggressive feelings may be transferred. Such transference relieves some of the tension related to the aggression and defuses the human relationships involved.

In the messages, John's apparent hostility to his opponents is transferred to the one like a son of man. Christ will make war with the sword of his mouth against the Pergamenes who follow "Balaam" and the Nicolaitans (2:16). The son of God will throw "Jezebel" into a sickbed and those who follow her he will throw into tribulation or strike dead (2:22–23).

In the fifth seal, the souls of the slain cry out for vengeance upon "those who dwell on earth" (6:10). This cry is a thin veil over the hearers' desire for vengeance on Rome. They do not fight Rome directly; rather, they pray to God to vindicate them. The aggression is transferred to God. In the sixth seal, the eschatological woes are described, including the rolling up of the sky like a scroll and the removal of islands and mountains. Naturally, all humanity is affected. Yet the depiction of distress focuses on the cries of the mighty, of kings, great men, generals, the rich and strong. The aggression of the powerless toward the powerful is expressed here. It is transferred to God and the Lamb. The last day is the day of *their* wrath.

In the second half of the book (chs. 12–22), vengeance is wreaked particularly against Rome. When the seventh angel poured out his bowl, the great city split into three parts and "God remembered great Babylon, to make her drain the cup of the fury of his wrath" (16:19). A great multitude in heaven is heard saying, "Hallelujah! Salvation and glory and power belong to our God, for his judgments are true and just; he has judged the great harlot who corrupted the earth with her fornication, and he has avenged on her the blood of his servants" (19:1–2). The hearers' hostility to Rome is transferred to another subject, namely, God.

In each of the cases in which aggression is transferred to another subject, it is also transposed from the present to the future. John the prophet was in conflict with "Balaam," with the Nicolaitans, and with "Jezebel" at the time Revelation was written. The aggressive feelings he probably felt were a matter of the present from his point of view. The resolution of the conflict, however, is presented indirectly as belonging to the future. The Christ of the message to the Pergamenes says, "I *will come* to you *soon* and war against them ["Balaam" and the Nicolaitans] with the sword of my mouth" (2:16; emphasis added). With regard to "Jezebel" and her followers, the threatened judgment by Christ is also future (2:22–23). The eschatological woes (6:12–17) and the destruction of "Babylon" (16:19) are events expected by John and the hearers in the near future. The announcements of these events are in the past tense only because they report John's visions. The visions took place in the past, but the events they foreshadow are yet to come. This transposition of aggressive feelings into imagined aggressive acts in the future is another way of alleviating the tension awakened by such feelings.

The second method of containing aggression reflected in Revelation is that of internalizing it and reversing it, so that it falls on the subject of the aggressive feelings. This process may explain the intensification of norms which the Apocalypse expresses and evokes. If John and some of the hearers turned their aggression inward, this would explain why they became more demanding of themselves and other Christians with regard to assimilation, wealth, sexuality, and the urge toward self-preservation.

The messages to Ephesus, Pergamum, and Thyatira oppose tendencies to assimilation on the part of some Christians. They thus intensify the early Christian norm of exclusivism with regard to Greco-Roman culture, especially its polytheistic aspect. The origin of this intensified norm in aggressive feeling is evident in the highly negative language used to describe the opponents themselves, with their teachings and practices, and in the violently threatening language used against them and their followers. As we have seen, the labeling of the rivals as "Balaam" and "Jezebel" already expresses John's thoroughgoing denunciation of them and their teachings. Their teaching itself is called idolatry indirectly and harlotry directly. It is difficult to imagine two more emotionally laden concepts for the time and place, naturally in the negative sense. Christ is presented as saying that he *hates* the works of the Nicolaitans and as approving of the Ephesians' *hatred* of those works. The judgment Christ will execute on these unrepentant opponents is described in very violent terms, as we have seen.

In Chapter 4, I argued that the message to the Laodiceans (3: 14–22) shows that John believed that under the circumstances Christians had to be at least detached from wealth, and that it was better to be economically poor. In Chapter 3, Revelation 18 was interpreted as a condemnation of wealth obtained or held by collaboration with Roman power. In Chapters 1 and 4, it was suggested that John was an itinerant prophet dependent on alms and hospitality. John's life and the book he wrote thus support that strand of early Christian tradition which is critical of wealth and idealizes poverty. As with the norm of exclusiveness, it seems that the implied idealization of poverty in Revelation has its origin in aggressive feeling, namely envy. We have seen how prominent gold, precious stones, pearls, and monumental architecture are in the vision of the new Jerusalem. In 5:12 it is proclaimed that the Lamb is worthy to receive power and wealth among other things. The Lamb's reception of them involves his followers too (5:10; 20:4–6; 21:24–26; 22:5). These elements show that wealth as such was not rejected in the Apocalypse. The problem was that the wrong people had power and wealth in John's situation. In order for the feeling of envy to be controlled, the possession of riches in the present had to be presented as evil and hateful in itself. This is done by linking wealth and pride: the Laodiceans are admonished as follows: "For you say, I am rich, I have prospered, and I need nothing; not knowing that you are wretched, pitiable, poor, blind, and naked" (3:17). More pointedly, Rome is accused of saying, "A queen I sit, I am no widow, mourning I shall never see" (18:7), in a context in which wealth is a major theme. It is also done by associating luxurious clothing and jewelry with drunkenness, harlotry, and even violence in the vision of "Babylon" in ch. 17. The list of cargo over which the wholesale dealers mourn consists, as we have seen, in large part of luxury items (18:11–13). The use of these goods is implicitly condemned by the subtle reproach of the last item: "bodies, that is, human souls" ("bodies" was the usual word for slaves).

In Chapter 4, I argued that Rev. 14:4 idealizes continence. As shown in the same chapter, a high value was apparently placed on sexual continence from the beginning in some strands of Christian tradition. Nevertheless, the attitude reflected in Revelation may have been an intensification of norms in relation to Christian practice in the region at the time. This hypothesis is supported by the fact that continence is not advocated for all, but only for those who would "follow the Lamb wherever he goes." Once again, there is evidence of an origin in aggressive feeling. Continence is presented, not so much as a positive good, but rather as the avoidance of a disturbing alternative: "It is these who have not *defiled* themselves with women." Such a remark reveals a complex set of emotions, involving perhaps hatred and fear both of women and one's own body.

The Jewish writers Philo (first centuries B.C.E. and C.E.) and Josephus (first century C.E.) admired the Essenes for practicing continence.[18] An intensified purity may well have been the Essenes' goal in the practice, but neither Philo nor Josephus emphasizes this rationale. Both of them speak of women in a highly stereotypical and misogynist way. Josephus comes closer to the idea of purity in saying that the Essenes avoid the danger of adultery by eschewing marriage.[19] He also states that they renounced pleasure as evil and held resistance to the passions as a virtue.[20] It is clear that Josephus has reinterpreted the logic of purity in ethical terms. Both Josephus and Philo argued that the Essenes avoided marriage because the relationships between husband and wife and husband and children undermined the commitment to other members of the group essential for communal life. Josephus says simply that they believed marriage to lead to discord.[21] Philo elaborates the idea at length.[22]

John's presentation of continence in Rev. 14:4 is strictly in terms of purity. The particular form the ideal of purity takes here is rather extreme. No positive aspect of sexual intercourse is mentioned or implied. Josephus clearly respected the need for the propagation of the human race.[23] The Gospel of Matthew recognized that intercourse was natural and in accordance with creation by speaking of the continent as eunuchs. There is no such ambiguity in Revelation. The hatred and fear of women apparently expressed in Rev. 14:4 probably have their roots in a negative attitude toward the body. Sexual intercourse and women are disturbing because they call to mind the vulnerability of a being with a body. Once again, an analogy with schizophrenia presents itself. According to Ernest Becker, the schizophrenic regards his or her body as something that "happened" to him or her. This attitude is simply a heightened awareness of something any human being might feel, as existentialist philosophers have shown. The schizophrenic views his or her body as a mass of stench and decay. This perspective is familiar also as the starting point of some forms of Buddhism. The schizophrenic takes this to an extreme, however, and feels that one's own body is only "a direct channel of vulnerability, the direct toehold that the outer world has on his [or her] most inner self. The body is his [or her] betrayal, his [or her] continually open wound, the object of his [or her] repulsion."[24] I do not mean to imply that the remark in Rev. 14:4 rises out of a technically pathological situation. It is however, a remark that demands critical assessment because of its potential for injustice toward women and alienation from the body.

The book of Revelation is an important stage in the process toward the glorification of martyrdom in parts of the early church. This incipient attitude is expressed in the remark that the blood of those slain for their faith would be avenged when the number of those to be slain was complete (6:11). Some desirous of vengeance on Rome might have been led by such a remark to sacrifice themselves to the cause. The remark that the 144,000 are firstfruits to God and the Lamb suggests, by way of the metaphor of sacrifice, that they are witnesses by blood as well as by word. The implication is that those who die for the faith form an inner circle around the Lamb. The glorification of faithful death is most clear in the vision of the messianic reign (20:4–6). The urge to faithful death is obviously the most extreme form of the internalization of aggressive feeling and its reversal toward oneself.

CONCLUSION

Through the use of effective symbols and artful plots, the Apocalypse made feelings which were probably latent, vague, complex, and ambiguous explicit, conscious, and simple. Complex relationships were simplified by the use of a dualistic framework. The Jews who reject and denounce Christians are followers of Satan. Those who do not have God's seal bear the mark of the beast and are doomed to destruction. Fear, the sense of powerlessness, and aggressive feelings are not minimized, but heightened. They are placed in a cosmic framework, projected onto the screen of the heavenly world. This intensification leads to catharsis, a release of the disquieting elements of the emotions in question. By projecting the tension and the feelings experienced by the hearers into cosmic categories, the Apocalypse made it possible for the hearers to gain some distance from their experience. It provided a feeling of detachment and thus greater control.

Dedication to the rigors of exclusiveness, poverty, continence, and faithful death can be seen as the internalization of aggressive feelings aroused by social tensions. The practice of these intensified norms provided a way of releasing some of the energy aroused by those tensions. To a considerable extent, however, the aggressive feelings were not eliminated, but were transformed into new kinds of aggressive feeling. The resentment due to the hostility of Gentiles toward Christians was internalized in part by calling for greater exclusiveness. But the intensified norm of greater exclusiveness led to a division among Christians and aggressive feelings toward those who rejected or failed to live up to the intensified norm. A similar process may have occurred with regard to wealth. This transformation of aggression raises the question whether the process of containing aggression reflected in the Apocalypse is appropriate and adequate. It is certainly not dysfunctional or maladaptive in a pathological sense. It was adequate in the sense that pathological behavior was apparently avoided and, as far as we know, the anger of John and some hearers did not erupt into violence against their non-Christian neighbors, a violence that surely would have worsened their situation. The process was inadequate in the sense that the cause of aggressive feelings was not dealt with and resolved so that aggression could be eliminated without giving up on the ideal of a sociopolitical transformation. It is doubtful that a full resolution was possible, but more realistic attempts to solve the problem could have been formulated. Whether the process was appropriate is a question which involves theological and ethical reflection. This last question will be discussed in the Conclusion.

NOTES

1. L. Festinger, *A Theory of Cognitive Dissonance* (Stanford University Press, 1957); John Gager, *Kingdom and Community* (Prentice-Hall, 1975), pp. 37–49.

2. Claude Lévi-Strauss, *Structural Anthropology* (Basic Books, 1963), p. 229.

3. Edmund Leach, "Lévi-Strauss in the Garden of Eden: An Examination of Some Recent Developments in the Analysis of Myth," in E. N. Hayes and T. Hayes (eds.), *Claude Lévi-Strauss: The Anthropologist as Hero* (Cambridge: MIT Press, 1970), pp. 50–51.

4. Lévi-Strauss, *Structural Anthropology*, p. 229.

5. G. B. Caird, *The Language and Imagery of the Bible* (Westminster Press, 1980), p. 7.

6. Ibid.

7. Adela Yarbro Collins, *The Combat Myth in the Book of Revelation* (Scholars Press, 1976); "The History-of-Religions Approach to Apocalypticism and the 'Angel of the Waters' (Apoc. 16:4–7)," *CBQ* 39 (1977).

8. Yarbro Collins, *The Combat Myth in the Book of Revelation*, Ch. 1.

9. Ibid., Ch. 5.

10. See the discussion in S. H. Butcher, *Aristotle's Theory of Poetry and Fine Art*, 4th ed. (Dover Publications, 1951), pp. 240–257.

11. Cited by Ernest Becker, *The Denial of Death* (Free Press, 1973), pp. 62–63.

12. Ibid., p. 63.

13. Quoted by Becker, ibid., pp. 25–26.

14. Ibid., p. 63.

15. Ibid., p. 76.

16. George De Vos, "Conflict, Dominance, and Exploitation," in Nevitt Sanford and Craig Comstock (eds.), *Sanctions for Evil* (Jossey-Bass, 1971), p. 171.

17. My thinking along these lines has been stimulated by Gerd Theissen, *Sociology of Early Palestinian Christianity* (Fortress Press, 1978), Ch. 9.

18. Philo, *Hypothetica* 14–17 (cited by A. Dupont-Sommer, *The Essene Writings from Qumran* [Peter Smith, 1973], pp. 25–26); Jose-

phus, *Jewish War* 2.120–121, 160–161; *Antiquities* 18.21 (Dupont-Sommer, pp. 27–28, 35, 36).

19. Josephus, *Jewish War* 2.121.

20. Ibid., 120, 161.

21. Josephus, *Antiquities* 18.21.

22. Philo, *Hypothetica* 14–17.

23. Josephus, *Jewish War* 2.121, 160–161.

24. Becker, *The Denial of Death*, p. 220.

Conclusion

The appropriateness of the historical-critical method for biblical texts has been called into question by those who feel that the "world in front of the text" should be the focus of attention, rather than the "world behind the text." The preceding chapters have shown that an accurate understanding of the "world behind" the Apocalypse is indispensable for an appropriate appreciation of the "world" created by the text itself. We have seen how historical, literary, and psychological methods of explanation complement one another in showing how the Apocalypse interpreted the social situation in which it was written and both expressed and elicited a response to it.

The "world behind the text" has been presented as the social situation in which the first hearers found themselves, as perceived and interpreted by the author, John the prophet. This situation has been described from various points of view. The most general aspect is the position of early Christians as members of Hellenistic Near Eastern peoples subject to the authority of Rome. Other aspects are the social relations and tensions between believers in Christ and the Jewish people, the religious, social, economic, and political situation of western Asia Minor, and the values and experiences of author and addressees. The evidence does not support the conclusion that the book of Revelation was written in response to an external crisis due to some recent historical or social change. The Apocalypse was indeed written in response to a crisis, but one that resulted from the clash between the expectations of John and like-minded Christians and the social reality within which they had to live.

The power of the Apocalypse lies in its ability to articulate this perceived crisis and to deal with it in an effective way. Its means of dealing with it is the creation of a new linguistic "world." By means of effective symbols and narrative techniques, the book of Revelation releases the tension aroused by the perceived crisis in a process similar to the phenomenon of catharsis which Aristotle discussed in connection with Greek tragedy. Much of the Apocalypse can be explained persuasively as literary means for dealing constructively with the aggressive feelings aroused by the perceived crisis. To some extent these feelings are diffused by transferring them to another subject, God or the Lamb, and by transposing them from present to future. Another means of dealing with aggressive feelings is reflected in Revelation, that is, the internalization and reversal of such feelings against the subject by means of intensified norms for the Christian way of life. These literary and psychological observations have shown in different but complementary ways how the Apocalypse interprets and responds to its sociohistorical situation.

We have seen that the Apocalypse dealt with the crisis perceived by its author in at least a somewhat effective way. Simply accepting Revelation's means of resolving the perceived crisis and immediately seeking to apply it analogously to some aspect of our own situation today would be a precritical response. If we wish to move beyond precritical reaction to the text, we must assess critically the Apocalypse's means of resolving tension. Such critical assessment is important because the experience of such tension is a perennial human experience and because Revelation's resolution continues to have influence due to the book's status as a canonical text.

It is difficult to reach consensus on what the criteria for critical assessment ought to be. The traditional view is that various portions of Scripture must be assessed in terms of their accordance with the rule of faith. This rule of faith finds expression in the doctrines of the church. The historical-critical movement challenged the doctrinal approach to the Bible. Historical critics evaluated biblical texts in terms of the values and criteria of scholarly disciplines, especially historiography. Biblical texts were assessed in terms of their congruence with critically reconstructed history.

One result of historical-critical study of the Bible has been the recognition of its diversity. If different biblical books express different, even at times contradictory positions, discovering the Bible's authoritative teaching has become a problem. Another result is the awareness of the differences between the perspective of any biblical text and any modern reader's perspective. Attempts to come to terms with these results have led to a new movement that focuses on biblical hermeneutics, that is, the attempt to interpret biblical texts in a responsible way.

Some participants in this movement are content to let the diversity in the Bible stand. Others have formulated a "canon within the canon," a biblical principle or portion of the Bible in accordance with which other parts of the Bible can be assessed. Most often this "canon within the canon" is the event of the exodus, the historical Jesus, or the Pauline gospel. Some have claimed that any "canon within the canon" is not critical enough. This claim has been made especially by feminists who perceive that the Bible as a whole, including the portrayal of Jesus, is patriarchal. They have proposed that authority not be presupposed for any part of the Bible, but that it be conferred on those passages or traditions which are conducive to the liberation of women.[1]

Some form of this position, in which authority is conferred, not assumed, is surely the only possible stance a person can take who wishes truly to be critical. Such a position is supported by the values of historical-critical scholarship. The only reliable guide in making judgments is the interpreter's or reader's own *critically interpreted* present experience. The words *critically interpreted* make an important contribution. It is not appropriate or helpful to assess biblical texts in terms of one's preferences without critical reflection on them. Both reflection on the hermeneutical process and on the procedure of making historical judgments have shown how crucial the historical situation of the interpreter or critic is. What one understands and how one judges depend on who one is. Liberation theologians have added the insight, following Marx and others, that the interpreter's social location also influences the resulting interpretation.

The implication of all this is that the book of Revelation will have different effects depending on who is seeking to interpret it and on the circumstances within which it is interpreted. Nevertheless, it does have certain intrinsic qualities and tendencies. It is clearly a text that is political as well as religious. Its tone ranges from conflictual to violent. As criteria for assessing the political stance and relational tone of the Apocalypse I propose the values of humanization, justice, and love.

These values have roots both in critically interpreted present experience and in the Bible. The concept of humanization comes from the contemporary social sciences. Becoming fully human involves recognition of both one's limits and one's potential: the limits of life as an organism and the potential of having a symbolic nature. Humanization is a process to be affirmed both for oneself and for others. This concept is congruent with the biblical account of creation: the human body ultimately from the earth, human life from the breath of God.

Justice is a concept shaped by modern political theory, ethics, and liberation movements. Its strongest biblical mandate is in the classical prophets. It involves an equitable distribution of opportunities and goods, material and spiritual. It involves the realization of a sense of significance for every individual, regardless of sex, race, or social class. It involves a sense of personal dignity and autonomy for individuals and for the groups with which they identify.

Love is primarily a biblical value that has its roots in the teaching of Jesus. Its content today is given by the values of humanization and justice. Self-love is commitment to the process of becoming fully human: self-assertion, seeking justice for oneself. Love of neighbor involves making the attempt not to prevent others from doing the same, and assisting them where appropriate.

Let us assess the attitude toward Rome in Revelation from the point of view of the values of humanization, justice, and love. As we saw in Chapter 4, the book of Revelation expresses and elicits uncompromising opposition to Rome. This opposition is expressed most vividly in chs. 17 and 18. These passages have offended the moral and religious sensibilities of many readers, believers and unbelievers alike. Revelation 17 depicts Rome in a highly unflattering light and ch. 18 describes the destruction of the city of Rome and of the political and economic system associated with it. The dirges of Rome's friends are interrupted in 18:20 by a call to rejoice: "Rejoice over her, O heaven and saints and apostles and prophets, because God has given judgment for you against her."

Most commentators attempt to justify the text in spite of the apparent offense. In commenting on 18:20, Bishop H. Lilje wrote:

> Because God executes judgment, the call for repayment must not be understood in the petty sense of human revenge. "Sancti sancto modo reddent"—"the saints 'repay' in a holy manner"—means that they are not animated by joy over destruction, but by certainty that God achieves his purpose, in spite of the arrogance of this secular power.[2]

Among the commentators it is perhaps William Barclay who has struggled most deeply with the harsh language of Revelation. In many of his comments he defends the text. A command to execute judgment on "Babylon" is contained in 18:6–8. With regard to this passage, he emphasizes that vengeance is not executed by human beings; vengeance belongs to God. Further, he argues that the passage "is not a case of grim, savage, harsh, vengeful law and justice; it is simply the expression of the great truth that every man is working out his own judgment."[3] Further, he argues that John's indictment of Rome was justified. He presents evidence of extremes of luxury, ostentation, gluttony, and waste. He points out that even Roman writers attacked this extravagant life-style.[4] On the other hand, Barclay is somewhat critical of portions of ch. 18. In verses 1–3 an angel is seen coming down from heaven, who announces judgment against "Babylon" in the form of a dirge. On this passage, Barclay declares, "It may be that we are far from the Christian doctrine of forgiveness; but we are very close to the beating of the human heart."[5] With regard to the call to rejoicing in 18:20, he frankly states that it "is not the more excellent way which Jesus taught." Perhaps by way of excuse, he reminds his readers that the call for rejoicing was written out of terrible suffering In spite of the element of vengeance, it is the voice of faith, of utter confidence that "no man on God's side could ultimately be on the losing side."[6]

Biblical scholars and theologians have been most concerned about the impression Revelation gives of a desire for revenge and the ethical and theological problems thereby raised. A somewhat different reading of the book was suggested by D. H. Lawrence, one which is, if anything, even more disturbing and challenging for the Christian who accepts Revelation as Scripture. He argued that the Apocalypse, especially chs. 12–22, is an expression of the anger, hatred, and envy of the weak against the strong, even against civilization and nature itself. Lawrence found the latter half of Revelation to be a rather boring historical allegory.

> Only the great whore of Babylon rises rather splendid, sitting in her purple and scarlet upon her scarlet beast. She is the Magna Mater in malefic aspect, clothed in the colours of the angry sun, and throned upon the great red dragon of the angry cosmic power. Splendid she sits, and splendid is her Babylon. How the late apocalyptists love mouthing out all about the gold and silver and cinnamon of evil Babylon! How they *want* them all! How they *envy* Babylon her splendour, envy, envy! How they love destroying it all! The harlot sits magnificent with her golden cup of wine of sensual pleasure in her hand. How the apocalyptists would have loved to drink out of her cup! And since they couldn't: how they loved smashing it.[7]

Elisabeth Schüssler Fiorenza has attempted to answer the criticisms expressed by exegetes like Barclay with regard to vengeance and those of Lawrence with regard to envy. She does so by taking the fifth seal (Rev. 6:9–11), the third bowl (16:5–7), the call to rejoicing (18:20), and the messianic reign (20:4–6) together as expressive of Revelation's theology of justice. In the fifth seal, the slaughtered cry out for justice and retribution; in the third bowl and the call to rejoicing, it is confirmed that the outcry has been heard and acted upon. Finally, 20:4–6 stresses the effect of God's judgment on those killed for their faith. She interprets the outcry of 6:9–11 as "the key question of people who suffer unbearable injustice and oppression: How long, O Lord?" She argues that many exegetes label this outcry as un-Christian and contrary to the preaching of the gospel only because they themselves "do not suffer unbearable oppression and are not driven by the question for justice."[8] She interprets the call to rejoicing in 18:20 as one of several signs that the author of Revelation was "clearly on the side of the poor and oppressed" and as an expression of "hope and encouragement for those who struggle for economic survival and freedom from persecution and murder."[9]

As we saw in Chapter 3, there is little justification for Barclay's excuse of "terrible suffering," which is probably meant in an objective sense. Likewise, it is doubtful that Schüssler Fiorenza can base her defense, as she attempts to do, on the assumption that John and his hearers were suffering "unbearable injustice and oppression." It is clear that justice is a higher value in the book of Revelation than love. The question is whether the circumstances at the time of writing justified the subordination of love to justice. The same question must be raised in any situation where any analogy to that of Revelation is perceived.

The dualist division of humanity in the Apocalypse is a failure in love. The division of all people into those with the mark of the beast and those with the seal of God is problematic also because of its lack of credibility. It is an oversimplification that eliminates not only the possibility of neutrality but also the complexities of life in which there are always shades of gray. But most important, this dualism is destructive and dehumanizing. One's enemies, including large numbers of unknown people with whom one supposes oneself to be in disagreement, are given a simple label, associated with demonic beings, and thus denied their full humanity. The act of denying others their full humanity diminishes the actor's humanity as well.[10]

The purpose of the Apocalypse seems to be the resolution of tension aroused by a perceived social crisis. As we saw in Chapter 5, some aggressive feeling was not contained constructively, but was transformed and directed against other Christians. In this transformation of aggression, we see a process similar to the dehumanization of non-Christian opponents as followers of the beast. The Christian rivals are also labeled and disposed of as an "out-group" by the use of the loaded allegorical names "Balaam" and "Jezebel."

This side effect, so to speak, raises the question of the long-term effectiveness of the Apocalypse's means of reducing tension. This effectiveness is questionable because of the use of violent imagery, its ambiguous effect, and the ambiguity of violence itself. As far as we know, the book of Revelation was written to avoid violence rather than to encourage it. The faithful are called upon to endure, not to take up arms. The violent imagery was apparently intended to release aggressive feelings in a harmless way. Nevertheless, what is cathartic for one person may be inflammatory for another. The same holds for various situations. Norman Cohn's book *The Pursuit of the Millennium* has shown that apocalyptic imagery has been linked historically to violence under certain conditions.[11]

It may be that violence is appropriate in some situations. Rollo May has written of life-giving anger and life-giving violence.[12] He had in mind individuals who live at a subhuman level, because of their lack of self-consciousness, assertiveness, and personal dignity. He argued that it may also at times be necessary for groups to resort to violence in the form of political rebellions to break out of their apathy and to force the dominant party to make social reforms.[13] For persons and groups living at subhuman levels, anger and violence may be constructive and life-giving, a step toward becoming more fully human. The violent imagery of Revelation and even the dualist division of humanity may be helpful in such situations. The passionate language and call to commitment can support a quest for personal dignity.

May also pointed out that the repressed anger of powerless people can erupt in unpredictable ways. It tends to erupt in all directions, even against the self. It is the eruption that is important; the aim or object can become secondary.[14] There is also a certain ecstasy in the experience of violence, a feeling that many people repress, but one that is difficult to control once it is unleashed.[15] These considerations suggest that the limited, rational use of violence in the quest for human dignity is a difficult achievement.

These considerations suggest that the political stance and conflictual tone of Revelation served the valid purpose of raising the consciousness of certain marginal and frustrated early Christians. Their commitment to a hope for the future that involved a transformation of the political and social order was a protest against the injustice of their current situation. The strength of the Apocalypse is the pointed and universal way in which it raises the questions of justice, wealth, and power. Revelation serves the value of humanization insofar as it insists that the marginal, the relatively poor and powerless, must assert themselves to achieve their full humanity and dignity. It is a book that expresses anger and resentment and that may elicit violence.

Its achievement is ambiguous insofar as aggressive feeling and violence can be destructive as well as constructive.

Revelation works against the values of humanization and love insofar as the achievement of personal dignity involves the degradation of others. The imagery of Revelation suggests a reversal of roles. Those who are now powerless and threatened will be powerful in the new order, whereas those who rule now will be powerless at that time. The Christ of the messages promises that he will give the conqueror "power over the nations, and he shall rule them with a rod of iron, as when earthen pots are broken in pieces" (2:26–27). He promises that the Jews who now reject the hearers will in future come and bow down before their feet (3:9). At the time Revelation was written, Christians were occasionally brought before Roman governors and condemned because of their Christian faith. The call to rejoicing in 18:20 envisions a situation in which these roles would be reversed. In the future, the Roman Empire would be on trial and condemned as now Christians are. At the time the Apocalypse was written the agents of Rome had power. In the reign of a thousand years and in the heavenly Jerusalem, the followers of the Lamb would have power and reign (presumably over others).

The imagery of Revelation thus does not suggest a new order in which all people will achieve personal dignity and autonomy. It may well be that such a vision would not have served well the need to encourage the marginal hearers to self-affirmation and assertion. Thus, the imagery and tone of Revelation may embody attitudes that are necessary in the struggle for justice under certain conditions. These attitudes, however, have a dark side of which interpreters of the Apocalypse must be conscious and whose dangers must be recognized. If Revelation's vision of the future is adopted, it must be in the full realization that it is a partial and imperfect vision.

The movement from a precritical to a critical reading of the Apocalypse involves the experience of its vision as a broken myth. The critical reader can no longer simply live and move and have one's being within the "world" of the text. A critical reading also leads to an awareness of how the text is flawed by the darker side of the author's human nature, which we, like all the readers, share. In spite of, and perhaps because of, these insights, we can move to a personal reinvolvement with the text on a new level. A postcritical reading is one in which a partial, imperfect vision can still speak to our broken human condition.

Since the book of Revelation is a book of visions and poetry, we should approach it first of all with our imaginations. Given its literary form, we should not approach it seeking information. Nevertheless, its symbols give rise to thought. By reflecting on the meaning and function of the symbols, we may discover their potential significance for us.

Meditation on the violent images, symbols, and narratives in the Apocalypse can have a variety of effects. Instead of ignoring or rejecting these portions as distasteful, one can use them as an occasion to discover one's own hostile, aggressive feelings. Critical reflection is then needed to determine the most constructive way of dealing with these feelings. It may be that they should be released in the imagination in a way analogous to Revelation's resolution of tension. Such an approach may be a step toward more self-assertive behavior. If such a process is not needed, a person may attempt to rechannel or defuse the aggression by imagining good things happening to the person or group with whom one is irritated. This approach may be helpful for those blocking the self-assertion of others.

As we have seen, power is a major issue in Revelation. Christ as lamb is overshadowed by Christ as judge and warrior. The significance of the kingship of God and Christ can be seen best by reflecting on what they oppose: the kingship of the dragon and the beasts, and the queenly rule of the harlot. The symbols of the dragon, the beasts, and the harlot give rise to thoughts on the nature of evil, on the nature of human sin. They make the impression that sin and evil are not just matters of individual choices. They suggest that individuals and even large groups of people can get caught up in collective processes with evil or destructive effects. They imply that there are trends, social structures, ideas, and institutional processes which are human creations, but which get out of human control and turn against their creator, like a Frankenstein monster.

Jacques Ellul and William Stringfellow have argued that this demonic quality inheres in all collective human realities, in all institutions, such as cities, corporations, nations, governments, and even the church.[16] This point of view seems to uphold the sovereignty of God at the expense of the dignity of humankind. It is probably true that all human institutions are to a considerable degree out of human control. As Peter Berger and Thomas Luckmann have argued, social institutions confront human beings as objective reality. But to call this objective, intractable quality demonic in all cases is going too far. Such an interpretation blunts the prophetic edge of the Apocalypse, which insists that the primordial forces of destructive power and death are embodied in *particular* institutions.

Social structures and collective processes become demonic at least under two conditions. When one group achieves or holds personal dignity and power at the expense of another group, the structures that support this situation are demonic. When an immediate objective or limited good is pursued without sufficient attention to the whole picture, the process can get out of control and become demonic. Examples of the first category are social structures that subordinate women to men and people of color to those who are white. An example of the second category is the development of nuclear weapons. Motivating forces were the joy of inquiry and discovery and the attempt to win the Second World War. The pursuit of scientific knowledge and technological capability had an inexorable logic of its own, especially in the climate of international fear and competition. The same forces have been at work in the buildup of nuclear arms by the two superpowers, forces that make it difficult to consider seriously what the common good may be.

Critical reflection on the symbols of the dragon, beasts, and harlot suggest that these and similar collective realities of our day are analogous to those demonic figures. The Apocalypse contains no specific program for meeting these challenges. It would seem, however, that collective forces must be dealt with collectively. Revelation thus supports the current trend in which the churches take public stands on social issues, a trend that is well established in the mainline Protestant churches, reviving in evangelical and fundamentalist circles, and now spreading to the Roman Catholic Church.

In Western European and American contexts where democracy is well established, the political theology of Johannes Metz seems to be a promising way of putting the imperative of Revelation into action. Metz does not base his approach on Revelation explicitly, but Christian hope for the future and the symbol of the kingdom of God play a significant role.[17] According to Metz, existential theology "correctly emphasized the role of the human person in contrast to the mere objectivistic viewpoint of scholastic theology. It has brought the Christian faith into a proper relationship to human existence and subjectivity."[18] But he sees two dangers in existential theology. It emphasizes the present at the expense of the future and the individual's journey of faith at the expense of "the social and political dimensions of the believer's faith and responsibility."[19] Metz's emphases on the future and on social and political dimensions of faith are also those of Revelation.

Metz proposes that the church be an "institution of a socially critical freedom."[20] Such a role is possible only if the church avoids being either a "ghetto-society" or an "ideological protective shell for

the existing society. Rather, it should become the liberating and critical force of this one society."[21] Further, the church can take this role
only if it develops a critical public within the church. This means that
some group within the church must take the responsibility of ques-
tioning and destroying the self-absolutizing tendencies of the church
as institution.[22]

In its role as an "institution of a socially critical freedom," the
church has two functions. One is to protest the absolutizing of any one
political program or system as the full achievement of the ideal social
order. Such a protest grows out of the "eschatological proviso," the
conviction that every stage that society has attained is provisional.[23]
The church must unmask the pretensions of ideologies. It must name
the beast. Secondly, the church should ally itself with those tendencies
in society which hold promise of a movement forward toward the
fulfillment of the eschatological promises of the Bible—freedom,
peace, justice, and reconciliation.[24]

There are, of course, significant differences between Revelation and
Metz's political theology. But Metz's proposal is one good example
of what an attempt to take Revelation both critically and seriously
might look like in the context of Western Europe or the United States
in the second half of the twentieth century.

NOTES

1. Elizabeth Cady Stanton, "Introduction," *The Woman's Bible*
(Seattle: Coalition Task Force on Women and Religion, 1974; originally published in 1895), pp. 7–13; Elisabeth Schüssler Fiorenza,
"Toward a Feminist Biblical Hermeneutics: Biblical Interpretation
and Liberation Theology," in Brian Mahan and L. Dale Richesin
(eds.), *The Challenge of Liberation Theology* (Orbis Books, 1981), pp.
91–112.

2. H. Lilje, *The Last Book of the Bible* (Muhlenberg Press, 1957), p.
234.

3. William Barclay, *The Revelation of John* (Westminster Press,
1960), Vol. 2, pp. 198–199; see also William Klassen, "Vengeance in
the Apocalypse of John," *CBQ* 28 (1966), pp. 300–311; G. Ernest
Wright and R. H. Fuller, *The Book of the Acts of God* (Doubleday
& Co., 1957), p. 337.

4. Barclay, *The Revelation of John*, Vol. 2, pp. 200–211.

5. Ibid., p. 195.

6. Ibid., pp. 213–214.

7. D. H. Lawrence, *Apocalypse* (Penguin Books, 1976; first published in 1931), pp. 87–88; see also pp. 114–115.

8. Elisabeth Schüssler Fiorenza, *Invitation to the Book of Revelation* (Doubleday & Co., 1981), pp. 84–85.

9. Ibid., p. 173.

10. Viola W. Bernard, Perry Ottenberg, and Fritz Redl, "Dehumanization," in Nevitt Sanford and Craig Comstock (eds.), *Sanctions for Evil* (Jossey-Bass, 1971), pp. 103–104.

11. Norman Cohn, *The Pursuit of the Millennium*, rev. ed. (Oxford University Press, 1970; 1st ed. 1957).

12. Rollo May, *Power and Innocence: A Search for the Sources of Violence* (W. W. Norton & Co., 1972), pp. 93–97, 137, 191–192.

13. Ibid., pp. 192–195.

14. Ibid., pp. 26, 95.

15. Ibid., pp. 165–167.

16. Jacques Ellul, *Apocalypse* (Seabury Press, 1977); William Stringfellow, *An Ethic for Christians and Other Aliens in a Strange Land* (Word Books, 1973).

17. Johannes Metz, *Theology of the World* (Herder & Herder, 1969), p. 25.

18. Ibid., p. 82.

19. Ibid., pp. 82–83; see also pp. 107–110.

20. Ibid., p. 134.

21. Ibid., p. 96.

22. Ibid., pp. 134–135.

23. Ibid., p. 153.

24. Ibid., pp. 92–96, 153.

Index